Presented To:

_____

From:

_____

Date:

_____

WISDOM *for* WINNERS

VOLUME THREE

WISDOM *for* WINNERS

VOLUME THREE

JIM STOVALL

AN OFFICIAL PUBLICATION OF
THE NAPOLEON HILL FOUNDATION

TO CLAIM YOUR ADDITIONAL FREE RESOURCES PLEASE VISIT SOUNDWISDOM.COM/NAPHILL

SOUND WISDOM
P.O. Box 310
Shippensburg, PA 17257-0310

For more information on publishing and distribution rights, call 717-530-2122 or info@soundwisdom.com

Quantity Sales. Special discounts are available on quantity purchases by corporations, associations, and others. For details, contact the Sales Department at Sound Wisdom.

While efforts have been made to verify information contained in this publication, neither the author nor the publisher assumes any responsibility for errors, inaccuracies, or omissions.

While this publication is chock-full of useful, practical information; it is not intended to be legal or accounting advice. All readers are advised to seek competent lawyers and accountants to follow laws and regulations that may apply to specific situations.

The reader of this publication assumes responsibility for the use of the information. The author and publisher assume no responsibility or liability whatsoever on the behalf of the reader of this publication.

ISBN 13 HC: 978-1-937879-69-3
ISBN 13 TP: 978-1-937879-89-1
ISBN 13 Ebook: 978-1-937879-70-9

For Worldwide Distribution, Printed in the U.S.A.
1 2 3 4 5 6 7 8 / 21 20 19 18 17

Cover/Jacket design by Eileen Rockwell
Interior design by Terry Clifton

CONTENTS

FOREWORD

PERHAPS YOU ARE ONE OF THE MILLIONS OF PEOPLE WHO HAVE enjoyed the 30 books written by Jim Stovall over the years. You may have even watched one of the movies that were made from Jim Stovall's books. Jim's best-selling book, *The Ultimate Gift,* with over five million copies sold, was one of the books made into a movie. *The Ultimate Gift* movie grossed over $110 million.

And perhaps you have read the first two editions of *Wisdom for Winners.* If so, you know the wit and wisdom that awaits you in this third volume—and you won't be disappointed. When Jim Stovall writes a column on wealth and life, he does so with authority.

Jim Stovall's *Wisdom for Winners* is a collection of columns that millions of people have read over the years. His wisdom and experience on a particular subject provide a great amount of credibility to his writings. Even though Jim has written several articles on overcoming adversity, perhaps for those who do not know his background, a little personal information is worth knowing. Jim aspired to be an NFL player and he had the mental and physical capabilities to be a success. Also, Jim was a heavy-weight Olympic weight lifter, but his plans took a serious challenge.

While attending Oral Roberts University, Jim was diagnosed with macular degeneration, which led to him becoming blind. Tutored by his girlfriend, Jim graduated. Most people going blind would just give up and seek government assistance. Not Jim. He told his dad (who was an employee of Oral Roberts University) that he wanted to work for himself. Jim's father introduced Jim to Lee Braxton, a large financial contributor to Oral Roberts University.

Jim was fortunate to be introduced to Braxton, as he was a great example of overcoming adversity and founder of many successful companies, including a bank. Lee Braxton was also a close friend of Napoleon Hill and delivered Hill's eulogy when he died in 1970. Braxton had used the principles found in Napoleon Hill's book *Think and Grow Rich,* and not only learned them, but took action. Braxton introduced Jim Stovall to *Think and Grow Rich,* which helped him become successful in financial and personal matters.

You will certainly be rewarded for reading Jim Stovall's columns on the value of wealth, learning is a life-long process, mastering your time, doing your best, looking for opportunities, what is important in life, and many other articles found in this volume of *Wisdom for Winners.*

While Jim's columns often provide financial advice, his columns also cover important topics such as "What is Important in Life." Jim gives advice on giving that creates a legacy for the giver. Jim tells us that while budgeting our money and making investments can benefit our family, it can also put us in a position to help others.

A favorite quote of mine from Stovall's *The Millionaire Map,* published by Sound Wisdom, simply states, "Never accept a map from someone who has not been where you want to go." If you would consider that simple statement and the good advice behind it, it could make the difference between you being successful, or just being one of the majority of people who are not.

Jim also wrote a book titled *The Financial Crossroads: The Intersection of Money and Life,* co-authored with Timothy J. Maurer, a certified financial planner. Jim reminds his readers that being motivated is useless if you do not know what to do. Knowing what to do is useless unless you are motivated to act.

Jim Stovall writes from his own personal experiences. For example, Jim has provided 500 scholarships for students attending Oral Roberts University. Jim has made many contributions, such as the articles you are about to read. Jim gave his many columns to the nonprofit Napoleon Hill Foundation to raise funds to provide scholarships for the University of Virginia's College at Wise. The Napoleon Hill Foundation also does prison work and has worked to make the success principles available around the world to make the world a better place in which to live.

I hope you enjoy the book, one column of wisdom at a time. Steve Forbes, publisher of *Forbes* magazine, calls Jim, "One of the most outstanding men of this era."

—**DON M. GREEN**, executive director of the Napoleon Hill Foundation, board member of the University of Virginia/Wise, and president of the University of Virginia/Wise Foundation.

TRUTH AND UNDERSTANDING

MOTHER'S DAY AND EVERY DAY

EACH YEAR AS MOTHER'S DAY APPROACHES, I REFLECT ON THE impact my mother has had and continues to have on me. This year, my thoughts are also drawn to a special mother who impacted her family and is now impacting the world.

As a novelist, TV and movie producer, as well as a platform speaker, I am always looking for great stories that will inform, educate, and inspire. As the old adage states, sometimes "Truth is stranger than fiction."

Each of my 30 books, the various screenplays I have written resulting in four movies, and hundreds of my weekly columns including this one, have been dictated to a talented colleague named Dorothy Thompson. Dorothy, in addition to being the best editor and grammarian in the business, has the patience and temperament to work with me when I'm attempting to be creative.

Several years ago, Dorothy received the alarming phone call that her elderly mother's health was failing. Dorothy immediately made the trip to another state to savor the last few days of her mother's life. In a conversation between Dorothy and her mother during that difficult but poignant time, Dorothy's mother—whose name was Joye—told Dorothy of a box on the top shelf of a closet in her home.

After Joye passed away, Dorothy and her sister took the time to fully examine the contents of that box. It was revealed that throughout her life, Joye had been a prolific and talented poet. Dorothy shared some of her mother's poetry with me, and as a writer myself, I was both amazed and envious of the quality and breadth of Joye's life's work.

After I reviewed the entire collection, I asked Dorothy and her family's permission to tell her mother's story and share her incredible poetry with the world. The result has been released in a unique and impactful book. You can get a free sample of Joye's work and learn more about this amazing story by visiting: www.DiscoveringJoye.com.

Beyond the book, my hope is to turn Joye's life and her work into a movie. It's one of those stories that, if I had simply made it up and put it in a novel or a screenplay, my publishers and the movie studios would have laughed aloud as they promptly deposited it in the trash.

To most people who knew Joye Kanelakos when she was alive, she was a good and decent person, but they were unaware of the hidden treasures inside. As you meet Joye through the new book and experience her transformational work, my hope is that you will plumb the depths of your own spirit and explore the treasures inside of you.

If you're looking for a wonderful gift for your mother or something to share with someone who has lost their mother, I hope you'll remember Dorothy's mother.

As you go through your day today, remember Mother's Day is celebrated once a year. Mothers are celebrated every day.

Today's the day!

THE POWER OF APPLAUSE

IN ADDITION TO MY WORK RUNNING A TELEVISION NETWORK, writing books, making movies, and writing weekly columns, several times each month, I get to speak at an arena event, convention center, or corporate meeting somewhere in the world. There are many things I enjoy about public speaking including getting to connect with a live audience, enjoying instant feedback, and getting to meet people as I sign their books or take photographs.

One of the elements of a huge arena event I had never understood before experiencing it myself was the overwhelming power of having thousands of people applaud for you. It causes you to want to be better, try harder, and give more.

Recently I read a story about the famed entertainer Jimmy Durante. At the end of World War II, many top performers were donating their time to entertain troops returning from the battlefields around the world. Durante was scheduled to perform for a group of wounded soldiers at a military hospital, but due to a scheduling conflict, Durante was forced to tell the commanding officer he only had five minutes before he had to catch a train for his next performance.

The commanding officer for the post was determined to make the best of a difficult situation, so he went onto the stage and introduced Jimmy Durante. Durante bounded onto the stage with his infectious energy, told jokes, and played a couple of his quick songs that he had made famous as a Vaudeville performer. At the end of five minutes, he took a bow to thunderous applause.

The commanding officer who was standing behind the curtain was surprised when Durante didn't leave the stage but launched into another series of jokes and songs. The crowd of wounded soldiers was overwhelmed when Jimmy Durante finally left the stage in complete exhaustion after performing almost two hours.

The audience showed its appreciation by giving Jimmy Durante a thunderous standing ovation. Backstage, the commanding officer asked Durante why he had continued performing and missed his train. Durante smiled and said, "It was the applause that did it."

Apparently the commanding officer looked bewildered, so Durante parted the curtain slightly so they both could see the crowd continuing to stand on their feet and applauding Durante's performance. The commanding officer was still confused until Jimmy Durante pointed out two soldiers on the front row. One of the soldiers had lost his left arm during the war, and the soldier sitting next to him had obviously had his right arm amputated. These two soldiers had apparently discovered that if they sat next to one another and combined their efforts, they could express their appreciation by applauding.

Durante said, "Trains come and go every hour, but an experience like that you get once in a lifetime."

While they may not be singers, comedians, or performers, the people in our lives need applause. Whether it's your friend, a family member, or a coworker, catch them doing something well, and let them know how much you appreciate it.

As you go through your day today, remember the power of applause works whether you're giving it or receiving it.

Today's the day!

PRIDE AND PERSPECTIVE

PEOPLE AROUND THE WORLD HAVE ADMIRED MUHAMMAD ALI
as a person and as a champion for decades. Ali took his talent
as a boxer and became a worldwide media icon. Anyone who
ever saw Ali fight or heard him interviewed probably heard him
loudly declare, "I am the greatest of all times." In more reflec-
tive moments, Muhammad Ali admitted that his statement was
designed to bolster his own confidence while creating doubt
and fear in the minds of his opponents.

You and I have to strike a delicate balance between confi-
dence and conceit.

Hillel the Elder was a Jewish leader during the reign of
Herod before the time of Christ. He said, "If I am not for
myself, who will be, but if I am only for myself, who am I?"
We all need to be fans of ourselves and of our work while
applauding the greatness in everyone and everything around us.

I'm in the television business, and our industry lives and
dies on rating points. These points determine how many peo-
ple are watching a particular program at a specific time. These
rating points are broken down into every conceivable demo-
graphic group, making it statistically possible for everyone to

be rated number one. While one network may boast they're number one among adult males, a competing network may be leading among females over 55, and still another network may boast they are top-ranked among left-handed Eskimos or some other absurd claim.

I believe it is important for you and me to always have something fixed in our minds for which we can be very proud while being mindful of other things in our personal and professional lives that need improvement.

My late, great friend and colleague Coach John Wooden often told me that you must guard against repeatedly practicing the thing you do best while ignoring the thing that needs your effort and attention. If you can celebrate the things that you do well, and keep them in perspective as you practice the areas that need improvement and relish your progress, you will become a champion at your chosen field.

Among any group of boxing experts or historians that might discuss the best fighter of any era, many will agree that Muhammad Ali was, indeed, "The greatest of all time."

As you go through your day today, become your own best fan and constructive critic.

Today's the day!

TALKING AND LISTENING

I REMEMBER AS A YOUNG CHILD BEING TOLD BY MY PARENTS and grandparents that I had two ears and one mouth, so I should listen twice as much as I talked. The fact that they had to repeatedly tell me this probably indicated that someday I would become a professional speaker.

We all need to listen—not only to what's being said but to how it's being said and to what's behind the words. There's a big difference between hearing, listening, and truly understanding.

I think it's interesting that the words "listen" and "silent" contain all of the same letters. My late, great friend and colleague Dr. Stephen Covey often said, "Seek first to understand and then to be understood." Dr. Covey recognized that in any conversation, debate, argument, or discussion, having both parties talking at the same time is counterproductive. He taught that you must first understand the other person's position and be able to articulate it to their satisfaction before you should begin to make your own point.

Ironically, I have found that when I practice this wisdom of Dr. Covey's, there is often very little difference between my opinion and the other person's. Somehow, the process of understanding someone else's words and the thoughts behind them allows us to reconsider our own position and discover a middle ground that had not previously been obvious.

As a blind person myself, people often ask me if my hearing is improved. Doctors have assured me that the acuity of blind people's hearing does not improve, but their listening skills become very acute. Just as there are things you might see but overlook, there are things we hear that we do not allow to come into our consciousness. Listening to others not only shows respect, but it gives us an opportunity to understand, learn, and create consensus.

Oftentimes, arguments, debates, or disagreements have more to do with semantics than reality. People fight to have everyone understand and agree with their description or verbiage surrounding an issue more than the position on the issue itself. In order to create harmony and consensus, we must give up the need to be right. As long as we divide the world into right vs. wrong, we force there to be a winner and a loser. Anyone who has a significant other in their life knows that you can win an argument and walk away a loser. Listening is a skill, an art, and a science. It is one of the critical elements of success.

As you go through your day today, commit to listen, hear, and understand, then decide whether or not you have anything to say.

Today's the day!

CONTENTMENT, COMPARISON, AND COMPLACENCY

MUCH OF WHAT WE SEEK AS WE STRIVE FOR THIS THING WE call success is actually contentment. Contentment is an elusive and complex state. To be content, we must accept things as they are but not necessarily accept the current condition as a permanent situation. Contentment comes only when we judge ourselves in light of who we know we should be and can be.

There is never any comparison involved in contentment. Contentment cannot be achieved if we compare ourselves to what other people do or what they may have. I find many unhappy people around the world failing in an attempt to reach someone else's goal. Only you can determine who you are and where you want to be.

While there is no comparison in contentment, there is also no complacency. Being content with where we are does not mean we are satisfied to stay in our current position. If you are taking a road trip from your home to a destination 200 miles away, as you reach the halfway point, you will have traveled 100 miles. You may be very content with your progress thus far as long as you don't compare it to your destination or become complacent and accept your journey half traveled.

Your academic performance as a fifth grader may have been judged exceptional, and therefore, your teacher gave you an A on your report card. If you compare yourself to students who didn't perform as well, you might become complacent and stop studying hard and doing the things it took to achieve an A on your report card. If you're performing as an A-level fifth grader when you arrive in the 10th grade, you will likely receive an F on your report card and fail the course.

We must find a balance between determining who we are and where we are without comparing ourselves with others or becoming complacent and accepting our current status.

Learning is a lifelong process, which is why I believe the graduation ceremony is called a commencement. A commencement means the beginning of a process, not the end.

If you had studied computer science and had become a leading authority in the world ten years ago or even five years ago, you could have achieved many things; but if you compared yourself to less-accomplished people at that time and became complacent, your five-year-old computer skills would be totally obsolete today.

The great mountaineer, Sir Edmund Hillary, had many failed attempts to reach the summit of Mount Everest. He felt each of these expeditions had achieved a certain level of success that he knew would eventually culminate in his reaching the top of the world. He became famous for giving speeches to raise money between his various attempts to climb the mountain.

On each occasion, he would stand in front of a giant mural of Mount Everest, and as he closed his remarks, he would turn and speak directly to the mountain, proclaiming, "I will eventually succeed because you can't get any bigger, and I can."

As you go through your day today, be content with where you are without comparing yourself to others or becoming complacent about the future.

Today's the day!

BOOKS AND PEOPLE

MY LATE, GREAT FRIEND, MENTOR, AND PUBLISHER CHARLIE "Tremendous" Jones was fond of saying, "You will be the same person you are today five years from now except for the books you read and the people you meet." When I first heard Charlie say this two decades ago, I thought it was significant. Today, I know it to be true; therefore, I wanted to take this opportunity to introduce you to two of my books.

The Ultimate Life novelization, which is the book version of the Twentieth Century Fox movie based on one of my novels, is now available. (Visit: http://ow.ly/xgaTH.) This is both the sequel and prequel to *The Ultimate Gift* book and movie. It will reintroduce you to some old friends, show you where they are going, and reveal where they have come from. And in case you missed the first and second compilation of my weekly columns put out by The Napoleon Hill Foundation, look for *Wisdom for Winners—A Millionaire Mindset* and *Wisdom for Winners Volume 2*.

If you ask top achievers in any field to give you a list of books that should be read in order to generate success, some of the titles will vary, but virtually every list will have a book from Napoleon Hill. I am very proud to be associated with The Napoleon Hill Foundation and very grateful for readers around the world who read my columns each week for creating the demand for a compilation of these weekly efforts in books.

As the best-selling author of 30 books with millions of copies in print, I'm embarrassed to tell you that when I could read with my eyes as you are reading these words, I don't know that I ever read a whole book cover-to-cover. But after losing my sight and discovering the National Library for the Blind with its audiobooks along with a high-speed player, I'm pleased to report that I read an entire book virtually every day.

I gave the keynote speech for the Library of Congress's national convention that included all of the librarians from the National Library for the Blind. I told them how those books changed a scared, young blind person into a successful entrepreneur, platform speaker, columnist, movie producer, and author. I'm excited that the process has come full circle, and my books, *The Ultimate Life* novelization, *Wisdom for Winners,* and *Wisdom for Winners Volumes 2 and 3*, will be offered in an audio format and made available through the National Library Service for the Blind.

When we learn something, we change our lives. When we teach others, we change their lives. But when we teach people to teach, we can change the world.

I hope you will continue to read my books and other titles that can make your life better, but I also hope you will share them with others as you encourage them to pass it on. In this way, we can change the world.

As you go through your day today, realize you can change the world by changing yourself through the people you meet and the books you read.

Today's the day!

What's in a Name?

When we meet a new person, the first thing they learn about us is our name. Our name, by itself, may not mean much in that initial meeting, but will come to mean a great deal to everyone we encounter throughout our lives.

Think of Neil Armstrong, Louis Armstrong, and Lance Armstrong. They all share the same last name, but we know them for different reasons, and their names evoke different thoughts and emotions. This is true, both in our personal and professional lives.

In the global economy, nothing is more valuable than a good name. Periodically, the ranking of the most valuable brand names in business is released. For several years the Apple Corporation had the most valuable corporate name in the world. One year Google took over the number one spot. Here are the top ten brand names in the world:

1. Google
2. Apple
3. IBM
4. Microsoft

5. McDonald's

6. Coca-Cola

7. Visa

8. AT&T

9. Marlboro

10. Amazon

Each of these names is familiar to virtually everyone. Their names may evoke positive or even negative thoughts in your mind, but each name is respected within the arena where these companies do business.

Consider Amazon in the last spot on the list. They do not manufacture products or provide services other than creating a worldwide gathering place for commerce. If you were to purchase Amazon, it would cost you billions of dollars to buy, and the majority of what you would get for your purchase price would be the right to use the name Amazon.

My late, great friend and mentor Coach John Wooden was fond of telling his players, "You will be known for a lifetime of great things you do or a momentary lapse in judgment." Your name means something to those around you. When people consider your name, they may think of you as reliable, trustworthy, and credible, or they may think of you in less flattering ways. You and I daily have the opportunity to either reinforce what our names mean to those around us or undergo an identity transformation and, literally, change who we are perceived to be.

I'm acquainted with a man who is habitually late. Whether it's a dinner, a business meeting, an entertainment event, or church service, he will invariably arrive late. If you talk to other people about him, his tardiness will generally come up within the first few moments of the conversation. This is not a good image to create; however, this individual can change that image of himself simply by making a conscious effort to be prompt over the next twelve months.

I'm amazed at how quickly you can rehabilitate your reputation. If you are known for being late and then show up on time, people will take undue notice of your promptness. It won't be long before people will be talking about it, and once they've experienced you being on time on several occasions and discussed it with those around them, it will become routine and ordinary. At this point, you will have effectively changed the image or meaning of your name.

The most valuable business name in the world is Google. They simply allow you to enter any business or person's name into your computer and determine what that name means to other people and what they are saying about it. You can have a worldwide reputation, and your name can be thought of in a good or bad light anywhere in the world without you having to leave your hometown.

Be aware of what your name means to others. If you are pleased with that image, nurture it—and if you're not, change it.

As you go through your day today, make sure your name means everything you want it to mean.

Today's the day!

DANCES WITH WOLVES

FOR MORE THAN A DECADE, MY WEEKLY COLUMNS HAVE BEEN read by countless people around the world in hundreds of newspapers, magazines, and online publications. People from every country, culture, and walk of life partake of my weekly visits. For this reason, I try to be universal in my perspective and keep my global audience in mind. But occasionally, there's a bit of wisdom from my own backyard that I feel will be relevant to those seeking a better life anywhere around the globe.

I live in the middle of the United States, in Oklahoma. If people around the world know Oklahoma for anything, it probably would involve a famous Broadway show, the oil industry, or our American Indian heritage. We have a very rich and varied Indian culture throughout Oklahoma.

Recently I had the privilege of hearing an elderly Indian gentleman tell a story his grandfather had shared with him over eight decades ago. Apparently this wise Indian grandfather told his grandson that there are two wolves that live inside each of us, and these wolves constantly fight one another. One of these wolves the grandfather described as good, noble, loving, giving, and successful. The second wolf he described as being bad, evil, manipulative, vindictive, and a failure. Upon hearing this, the grandson was reportedly prompted to ask his grandfather, "Which wolf wins the fight?" The grandfather provided the young boy with wisdom that served him well throughout his life and can be equally impactful to you and me. In answer to the question, "Which wolf wins the fight?" the grandfather simply and profoundly answered, "The wolf you feed."

As you may know, in addition to writing weekly columns, authoring books, producing movies, and making speeches, I am in the television business. In the TV industry, there are two diverse and opposing messages. This is what the Indians would describe as "speaking with a forked tongue." The television industry on the programming side dismisses concerns about all of the violence, degrading images, and negative content as only make-believe and assures us that it really doesn't have an impact. On the other hand, this same TV industry on the advertising side will assure you that if you will spend several million dollars for a minute of commercial time, you will be able to sell multiple millions of dollars of whatever product or service you might market.

As the wise Indian grandfather well knew, whatever images we feed in our minds will, inevitably, grow and flourish in our lives. One of the most profound psychological principles involves the fact that we become what we think about all day.

As you go through your day today, commit to feeding the wolf you want to flourish and starving the one you wish to eliminate.

Today's the day!

PICK A LANE

DUE TO MY TRAVEL SCHEDULE, I FREQUENTLY FIND MYSELF IN airports across the country waiting to go through the security line. I have noticed a phenomenon among fellow travelers that involves getting in a line and then observing another line moving faster. They will invariably rush over to that line and stand there until once again they believe that another line is better. Regularly, the people who were in the original line and stayed put get through security much faster and are well on their way to their gate before these opportunistic line jumpers clear security.

You have probably noticed this same phenomenon in traffic when the car next to you at a stop light revs their engine and races away the microsecond the light turns green. They will weave in and out of traffic and screech to a halt at the next red light where they are predictably a few feet away from you again.

While this practice may be merely annoying in traffic or at the airport, the principle behind it can be critical in our personal and professional lives.

Experts and pundits often argue about the best field, career path, or business in which to be involved given current economic conditions. I'm a firm believer that people with passion in any field of endeavor can succeed better than they would in a field where they do not have passion; therefore, it is important that you pick the right lane for your life's work.

Several years ago, I spoke at a national convention for surgeons. These men and women had dedicated many years of their lives and countless hours of training to become qualified to be a physician and specialize as a surgeon. I was shocked when talking to several of the surgeons as I was signing their books that many doctors are not happy in their careers and wish they had pursued another path. This is sad as many doctors do not even begin their practice until they are well into their 30s and often feel trapped because of their student loan debt and the years they have invested in education and training.

I read that a jet airliner traveling from coast to coast across the United States will burn 80 percent of its fuel just to reach cruising altitude. This is true in our lives in that most career paths or business ventures require a tremendous amount of education, training, and investment in the beginning and then, those who have endured, generally enjoy reaping great returns for the time and energy they have invested.

Never confuse a job with a career. A job is something you take in order to pay the bills. This is important, honorable, and necessary; however, a career represents your passion, your purpose, and the contribution you will make to our world. You must choose it wisely and well.

As you go through your day today, choose your course wisely, then pursue it with passion.

Today's the day!

ALWAYS MOVE FORWARD

IF YOU REMEMBER ANYTHING FROM YOUR GEOMETRY CLASS IN school, it's probably the fact that the shortest distance between any two points is a straight line. Moving forward along that straight line always represents the most efficient, productive, and profitable course of action, assuming that you have picked your destination point wisely.

I heard about the artwork in the design on an Australian coat-of-arms. There are two animals indigenous to Australia that appear on that coat-of-arms. They are the kangaroo and the emu. These two animals aren't too much alike, but they do share one unique characteristic. Because of the length of their tails, kangaroos cannot back up. If they want to reverse course, they have to move forward and execute a U-turn. Because of the configuration and shape of their feet, emus cannot back up and must always move ahead. The wise person who designed this particular Australian coat-of-arms understood that we can learn a lot from emus and kangaroos.

As we pursue our passion and move toward success, there are days when the forward progress is evident to everyone around us. Then there are other days when the progress is not evident to the casual observer. This could mean that no progress was made, or it could mean that you are moving forward in ways that do not reveal themselves immediately.

General George Patton often reminded his officers that he never wanted to receive any messages from the front stating, "We are holding our position." Patton believed that armies either moved forward or retreated. If you are currently stopped in one location, you must be making preparations and plans to move forward so that there is no time wasted or energy expended that does not result in progress.

If you have a goal, a dream, or a destiny in your life that you would like to reach, you should be making progress toward it today. That progress may involve taking significant strides toward those things you want to be, do, or have, or it may simply mean reading a book, meeting a person, improving your attitude, or any number of things that can put you in the right position to move forward immediately when the opportunity presents itself.

My late, great friend and colleague Dr. Stephen Covey taught a principle he called "sharpening the saw." Dr. Covey told about lumberjacks working in the forest energetically using their saws to cut down trees. These lumberjacks were paid based on how many trees they cut down in a day, so they worked very hard and consistently; however, seasoned and successful lumberjacks come to learn that there is a time when the fastest way to cut a tree down is to stop sawing and take a moment to sharpen the saw.

When you consider your life's work and your goals, you are the saw. There are times you will be rapidly moving toward your goal, and there are times when you are preparing yourself for the next big flurry of progress.

As you go through your day today, always be moving forward or preparing yourself for your next move.

Today's the day!

Entrepreneurial Efficiency

THERE IS A CERTAIN EFFICIENCY, EFFECTIVENESS, AND ECON-omy that comes with all entrepreneurial ventures.

I'm reminded of the stories recounted about the pilgrims who, upon arriving in the New World, began collective farming to try to feed themselves. Their thinking was that if they had one big farming operation and everyone shared the work and the harvest, it would provide the best outcome for all. I would have to admit that in theory and on paper a collective approach, or communism, makes a certain amount of sense and has an odd appeal; however, it quite simply doesn't work.

After nearly starving to death for several years, the pilgrims, in desperation, tried another approach in which each family would farm their own land and survive or starve based on their own harvest. They found that people were willing to work harder, smarter, and more efficiently for themselves and their families as opposed to the collective community.

The result was the individual families prospered, and many of them had enough surplus crops to share with families that needed help. Some might argue that this is an old-world example and doesn't apply in the 21st century. Consider the entrepreneur Elon Musk, best known for his cutting-edge, high-tech electric car, Tesla. Through Tesla, Elon Musk has planted the seeds that will change the transportation industry for generations to come.

In another venture with his company called SpaceX, Musk replicates the lessons learned and principles proven by the pilgrims. Space travel has been around in one form or another for over half a century. The established model involves a large rocket filled with fuel that blasts a capsule beyond the earth's atmosphere into space. Historically, the rocket itself was designed to be disposable and would fall away in stages as the fuel was consumed and the flight progressed.

Enter Elon Musk, an entrepreneur spending his own money earned from other entrepreneurial ventures. Immediately realizing that disposable rockets wasted untold millions of dollars, Musk and his engineers developed a rocket that remains intact and returns to earth by lowering itself much as a helicopter does as it lands. Through this development, Musk can reuse his rockets, cutting costs dramatically, and make it possible for his spacecraft to land almost anywhere and be reused many times.

I do not necessarily believe that Elon Musk is smarter than the many engineers and scientists around the world who pioneered and developed space travel. Musk's breakthrough comes from the advantage he gained from being an entrepreneur. Previous scientists focused on what was possible. Elon Musk and his team focus on what is possible as well as what's affordable, what's efficient, what's economical, and what is profitable.

As you go through your day today, think like an entrepreneur and enjoy the advantages.

Today's the day!

FREEDOM AND CIVILITY

NOTES FROM NAPOLEON

AMONG OTHER GENRES, I ENJOY READING BIOGRAPHIES AND history books. It's easy to learn from true stories because you know the ending as the narrative is unfolding.

Napoleon Bonaparte is one of the most complex historical figures of all time. You can find much to admire and to lament about Napoleon. I am fond of his words as he was preparing to cross the English Channel in his attempt to conquer England. He said, "The world belongs to those who know how to seize it."

Seizing the opportunity is often easier said than done because opportunities do not come giftwrapped and labeled as opportunities. A great opportunity for one person may not be an opportunity for another. For this reason, the most valuable preparation and planning you can do in your personal or professional life is to define the parameters of opportunities you are seeking. Success breeds success and attracts more success if you can only recognize it.

When I started out as a young, broke, struggling, aspiring entrepreneur several decades ago, I probably only reviewed one opportunity per month. Today, I am presented with several opportunities per hour when you consider all of the phone calls, emails, meetings, and direct mail. This can only be managed if I pre-identify and define what I seek.

I'm a firm believer in a concept I call "Accelerating your point of failure." If I can spend a few moments with a potential opportunity or venture and determine it is not appropriate for me, I consider this a success as opposed to launching an ill-advised project only to find out a year from now that it wasn't a good fit.

Sometimes, it's easier to define what we don't want rather than what we do want. This is a good initial weeding-out step. Here are a few criteria I use to quickly evaluate and eliminate many proposals from my consideration.

1. I do not get involved with projects that are illegal, immoral, unethical, or those my team and I cannot be proud of.

2. I do not get involved in projects that I do not understand or are not in my area of expertise or experience.

3. I do not get involved with projects involving people I cannot trust or those who have an unsuccessful track record.

4. I do not get involved in projects in which my unique talents and abilities are not required and highly valued.

With these four simple criteria, I can eliminate the majority of clutter, noise, and distraction in my business day and focus on the opportunities that earn and deserve my attention.

As you go through your day today, accelerate your point of failure, and you will speed toward success.

Today's the day!

FREEDOM, FREE SPEECH, AND TOLERANCE

YOU AND I, AT THIS VERY MOMENT, ARE ENGAGING IN ONE OF the most sacred privileges afforded by freedom. From the beginning of recorded history, the vast majority of people who have inhabited this planet never had the privilege of experiencing freedom of speech, freedom of expression, or the freedom to assemble.

Many of us who live in a free society take for granted the privilege of expressing our thoughts and gathering with others to engage in debate, discourse, or dissention. I am grateful to hundreds of newspapers, magazines, and online publications around the world that provide me a platform each week to express my thoughts, feelings, and opinions.

I believe, to the greatest extent possible, civil rights should be enjoyed and protected in a civil manner. The ability to disagree without being disagreeable is a gift that we can give to all free people. We can disagree with someone's words, thoughts, or opinions without diminishing them as a person.

Tolerance is a bridge between people of different viewpoints. If we blow up the bridge simply because we disagree with a position held by another, we cut off all communication and eliminate the possibility of creating consensus. I believe it is far better to fully communicate, and when necessary, agree to disagree on a particular issue while seeking common ground and finding topics where we can agree, support one another, and work together.

This type of conscious consensus happens best in a crisis. If you consider the allied forces during World War II, you will realize that a united coalition of people from different countries and of diverse race, religion, and political persuasion all came together to defend and preserve freedom around the world.

At the end of World War II, the differences among the allies surfaced once again, and a cold war emerged. While there were many differences, discussions, and disagreements, hostility was avoided, and the lines of communication remained open to the greatest extent possible. That struggle culminated in the immortal words felt in the hearts of all advocates of freedom but spoken by Ronald Reagan, "Mr. Gorbachev, tear down this wall." As you know, after Mr. Reagan said it, Mr. Gorbachev did it, and the Berlin wall remains a distant memory but potent reminder that things that separate and divide us can, eventually, be overcome as long as dialogue and diverse feelings are exchanged.

Freedom of speech, by its very definition, must extend to speech with which we disagree. This is what makes liberty an ongoing effort in understanding and tolerance. When you use this hard-won freedom of speech given to us by our ancestors as a weapon to attack someone's personhood instead of their position or political persuasion, you dishonor the sacrifice that made freedom of speech possible.

If you can exercise your civil rights civilly and deploy your freedom of speech respectfully, you will often discover that beyond an argument or debate there is a fellow lover of freedom willing to sacrifice to insure your freedom.

As you go through your day today, debate policy and love people.

Today's the day!

ALWAYS A MAVERICK

IN JULY 2014, I RECEIVED THE SAD BUT NOT UNEXPECTED NEWS that my hero, colleague, and friend James Garner had passed away. Future generations will remember Mr. Garner for his starring roles in countless films, his hit TV show *The Rockford Files*, as well as his signature role that propelled him to stardom in *Maverick*.

James Garner was not only a maverick on television. He was a maverick in his life. He was born in a tiny town in my home state of Oklahoma during the Depression and Dust Bowl era; however, he became an enduring presence in Hollywood without ever losing touch with his rural, mid-America roots.

He received two Purple Hearts as he served with valor during the Korean War but rejected movie and TV roles that portrayed gratuitous, senseless violence. Whether he was Maverick, Rockford, or one of his many movie roles, James Garner preferred to outwit his opponents as opposed to outshooting them.

Mr. Garner was a star in every sense of the word to several generations and people around the world, but he never lost the common touch or failed to be approachable and grateful for his success.

My career took a quantum leap when James Garner agreed to play Red Stevens in *The Ultimate Gift* and *The Ultimate Life*. His performances in those films proved to be his last two appearances on the silver screen. It seems somehow fitting that Mr. Garner's role as Red Stevens involves him playing a character who has already died before the story begins and relates how a person can pass on their values and life lessons after they are gone.

Mr. Garner's work will endure as long as people sit in front of a big screen or small one seeking escape, entertainment, and enlightenment.

In our brief association during the production, promotion, and distribution of two movies, Mr. Garner was struggling with a debilitating illness that eventually took his life; but he never let his condition affect his attitude, demeanor, or performance. If you want to see a true professional at work, find a copy of *The Ultimate Gift* DVD and watch James Garner as Red Stevens near the end of the movie tell his grandson, Jason, goodbye for the last time. That scene was done in one take as a continuous shot in which James Garner showed our cast and crew what it means to be a movie star.

As Red Stevens, James Garner taught his grandson and millions of moviegoers twelve life lessons he labeled The Ultimate Gift. The one among the twelve lessons I will always keep with me as an enduring memory of James Garner is gratitude. He took my words on a page and a character in my mind and brought Red Stevens to life.

As you go through your day today, follow the lead of James Garner and be a maverick.

Today's the day!

WISDOM FOR WINNERS

FOR ALMOST 20 YEARS, I HAVE BEEN PRIVILEGED TO WRITE COL-
umns each week and have them read by countless people around
the world in newspapers, magazines, and online publications.
On one previous occasion, a compilation of these columns was
gathered together in a book that was well-received and continues
to find success in the marketplace.

I was excited when Don Green, the head of The Napoleon
Hill Foundation, contacted me to do a compilation book entitled
Wisdom for Winners. Mr. Green wrote the Foreword to the book
and divided a number of my columns into individual sections
encompassing areas of personal and professional life.

We live in a world in which we are constantly bombarded by
countless images and messages on a daily basis designed to get
us to act in certain ways, buy certain products, and think certain
thoughts in order to benefit others; it is, therefore, imperative that
we control our own thoughts and actions through the input of
positive messages designed to move us toward our own success.

I am proud, pleased, and humbled to be associated with
Napoleon Hill in *Wisdom for Winners* and *Wisdom for Winners
Volumes 2 and 3*, which offer readers small, bite-sized messages

that can be read in a few minutes each morning or at a point during the day when a specific message is called for. Many Fortune 500 executives have read the same books, but the title most cited by these elite performers was Napoleon Hill's book *Think and Grow Rich*.

As a young man, Napoleon Hill approached Andrew Carnegie, the first billionaire, and asked about the key to success. Instead of giving some routine or flippant answer, Carnegie agreed to sponsor Napoleon Hill on a quest to find the keys to achievement and launch the science of success. Carnegie introduced young Napoleon Hill to Thomas Edison, Henry Ford, and dozens of the business leaders of the day. This collective wisdom emerged in Hill's 1937 classic book *Think and Grow Rich*.

Many of the people Napoleon Hill interviewed found their success in the 19th century, Hill compiled and wrote about it in the 20th century, and this timeless wisdom is available to you and me in the 21st century.

Now it is very exciting for me to have a group of these weekly columns compiled into three volumes entitled *Wisdom for Winners* released under The Napoleon Hill banner with Forewords by my friend and the head of The Napoleon Hill Foundation, Don Green.

I hope you are enjoying this third book as a way to launch or reenergize your own quest for success.

As you go through your day today, remember, you become what you think about, so commit to applying *Wisdom for Winners* in your own life.

Today's the day!

SEED OF LEADERSHIP

ONCE UPON A TIME THERE WAS AN ELDERLY, BENEVOLENT KING who had served and led his people well for many years. As all good leaders do, the king was aware of his own mortality and was planning for the day he stepped down from the throne. As this king had no heir, the law of the land called for him to appoint the next king.

When he knew the time was right, he called all of the elders and servants of the castle to the throne room and told them, "One year from today, I will end my reign as your king, and on that day I will appoint the new ruler of our land."

Gasps of surprise and murmurs of speculation could be heard throughout the throne room. The king waited until he had regained everyone's attention and stated, "I am giving each of you one seed to plant and care for over the next year. One year from today, each of you will reconvene here in the throne room to show what harvest you have gleaned from the seed I am giving to you this day."

Each of the elders, in turn, took a seed from the sack that the king held before him. Then the servants came forward, and each received their seed. Among the last of the servants to approach the throne was a young footman named Phillip. He bowed respectfully, took a seed from the bag held by his king, and rapidly left the throne room.

Phillip rushed home to his humble cottage that he shared with his young wife. Phillip showed his wife the seed he had received and told her of the king's plan to select the next ruler. Phillip cleaned their best clay pot, filled it with the most fertile soil he could find, and lovingly planted the seed he had been given. Over the next weeks and months, Phillip and his wife lovingly watered and fertilized the seed, but alas, nothing seemed to be growing in the pot.

While performing his duties in the castle, Phillip heard the other servants and elders bragging and boasting of the voluminous, colorful plants they were cultivating. Phillip and his wife were dejected, but they meticulously cared for the seed in the pot for the rest of the year.

On the appointed day, all of the king's elders and servants reconvened in the throne room to present their plants to the king and await his decision as to who would be his successor. The king commented on the lavish and healthy plants everyone had grown, and when it was Phillip's turn to come forward, he was embarrassed to set before the king an empty pot. The other servants and elders laughed and jeered at Phillip's obvious failure.

The king stood and raised his hands for silence, then announced, "I am pleased to turn my throne and the leadership of our land over to my honorable and dedicated servant, Phillip."

Everyone gathered in the throne room stood in stunned silence until the king explained, "One year ago, I gave each of you a seed. All of the seeds had been boiled. They were dead and unable to produce any of the plants you have presented here today. Phillip deserves your allegiance and your honor as he has demonstrated the first and most important element of leadership—that of honesty and integrity."

As you go through your day today, plant honesty, and you will live happily ever after.

Today's the day!

STAYING CLOSE FROM AFAR

WE LIVE IN A HUGE WORLD THAT IS SHRINKING IN MANY WAYS. It is easier than ever before to stay in touch with those we are close to, and it is simpler than ever before to meet new people and grow close to them via technology. I have written several books with very talented friends and colleagues I have never met face to face. Young people have grown up with technology and will actually sit in the same room and text one another instead of speaking aloud. While this may seem absurd to their parents or grandparents, it is part of our modern reality.

There are many definitions of success and many elements of success that make up each definition. Anyone's idea of personal success would have to include having quality, ongoing relationships with family and friends. Technology allows us to stay connected when we're not in the same town, state, or even country. Personal connection does not require personal contact.

By virtue of the fact that you are reading these words in a newspaper, magazine, or online publication, you likely have two functioning eyes. Let us consider the relationship between your two eyes. Your eyes blink together, move together, they cry together, see things together, and they even sleep together, but they never see one another directly. Your eyes can help you to see the whole world, but without benefit of a mirror or similar tool, you cannot see your own eyes nor can they see one another. A modern-day friendship or family connection can be much the same.

Our ancestors who lived in distant lands had to depend on an archaic mail system that often took months or even a year or more to deliver one piece of correspondence to a loved one. While a phone call may not be as good as an in-person visit, and an email may not be as good as a phone call, and a text may not be as good as an email, it's certainly better than nothing; and if it is heartfelt and meaningful, it can improve someone's day and even their life.

I have friends around the world with whom I correspond regularly, and our original connection came through my weekly columns. Like most things in our lives that are valuable, you've got to do them on purpose and not leave them up to random whims. You wouldn't go to a grocery store without a list of things you want to get lest you waste your time. How much more important is it that we not go through our lives without an ongoing list or calendar of people we want to stay in touch with and have as a part of our lives.

As you go through your day today, stay in touch, and you will give and receive one of life's most precious gifts.

Today's the day!

FACTS AND FANTASIES

Identifying Success

We live in a consumer society. We are judged and mea-sured based on what we buy, how often we buy, and everything we have. There are countless promotional and advertising images thrust upon us daily designed to make us feel inade-quate so that an imaginary heretofore unknown shortcoming in our lives can be solved by someone's product or service they want to sell us. We are told emphatically that we will be suc-cessful if we drive the right car, drink the right beverage, or use the right fragrance.

Success is not that simple, or maybe it's not that complex. Success is a self-fulfilling prophecy. No one else can define your success any more than they can order your dinner, try on a suit of clothes for you, or tell your doctor where it hurts. When it comes to your personal and professional success, you determine the destination, the deadline, and the details. No one else can do this for you, and you must identify and define your own success if you ever hope to achieve it.

When you want to tune in a certain radio station on a particular frequency, you adjust your radio to get rid of all the static and tune out the competing signals. Defining your own success is similar in that you must first get rid of all the noise and remove all the influences that do not come from your own mind, heart, and soul. If it is your passion and definition of success to become a special education teacher but you listen to messages from well-meaning family and friends urging you to become a corporate CEO, you may find yourself running a massive organization while making millions of dollars and living your life as an abject failure.

In the famous scene in *Alice in Wonderland*, the Cheshire Cat is asked which path to take. The wise cat inquired, "Where do you want to go?" When the response was, "I don't know," the cat stated for the moment and for history, "Then it really doesn't matter which path you take."

You can't achieve a goal you don't own. It doesn't matter what others think you should do, ought to do, or might do. All that matters is what you want your life to look like. Often this process begins with thinking of your perfect day and what activities bring you contentment. Then if you will consider paths that bring you more contentment and eliminate the things you don't want your days to look like, you will begin to piece together the puzzle that can define your own success.

As you go through your day today, remember there is no success in your life unless it is your own success.

Today's the day!

LEAVING A LASTING LEGACY

RECENTLY I RECEIVED A MESSAGE FROM ONE OF THE COUNT-less readers of my weekly column. The reader told me a dear friend of his had just passed away, and the reader was inquiring if I had any words of wisdom to share with friends and family at the memorial service. While I don't have any profound words that can make pain and suffering magically go away when the death of someone close occurs, I did share with that reader—and now want to share with you—my brief thoughts that seem to encapsulate how we should live our lives and leave our legacy.

I responded to that grieving reader as follows, "I am sorry for your loss. The best advice I could give you or those gathered at a service is that your friend's legacy consists of the things you have gained from your time together and how you will apply them in your lives going forward. We are all the sum total of the experiences we have had with friends and loved ones. Our tribute to them is how we live our lives, and the impact they have had is their legacy. I hope this helps."

Too many people believe that a legacy is something we concoct or formulate at the end of our lives. They think of it as some wise words or deep insight that we can leave behind in a few brief paragraphs in our last will and testament. In reality, our legacy is being built one day at a time, one act at a time, and one encounter at a time. There are people you will meet today who you will never see again. That brief encounter will be your legacy to that individual.

My late, great friend and mentor Coach John Wooden often instructed his players, "You will be known for a lifetime of good things you do or for one brief lapse in your conduct." I believe Coach Wooden understood and wanted his players to realize that some people will only be exposed to our weakest moment or our worst behavior. This is why Coach Wooden was also fond of saying, "Make today your masterpiece."

When we really understand the significance of everything we do, every word we say, and every person we encounter, we can do no less than our best in every situation.

As you go through your day today, realize that history is unfolding, and your legacy is being created.

Today's the day!

BEGINNINGS AND ENDINGS

IN ADDITION TO WRITING WEEKLY COLUMNS AND MY MOTIVA-
tional, success, and financial books, I enjoy writing novels and
working on the process of having those novels turned into mov-
ies. To date, four of my novels have been turned into films with
two more in production and scheduled for release next year.

Novels and movies are clear, concise, and finite. There is a
beginning, a middle, and an ending. These stories allow us to
encapsulate slices of life in a manageable format so we can be
informed, entertained, and hopefully, inspired. Real life is not
nearly so simple.

I am fond of Winston Churchill's statement during the
height of World War II. The prime minister said, "This is not
the end. It is not even the beginning of the end. But it is, per-
haps, the end of the beginning."

In my travels to make speeches in arena and corporate
events, I get to meet many people seeking success in their
personal and professional lives. They often refer to the begin-
ning or ending of their success quest with statements such as,
"Next week I'm going to begin pursuing a new goal that will
make me successful" or "Once I reach that point, I will truly

be successful and know that I have arrived." In reality, success has no beginning or ending. Goals are simply a means to compartmentalize our activity so we can measure our progress and performance.

In each of our personal and professional lives, we have thousands of activities, relationships, and projects going on all the time. New projects and goals begin as others end, only to be replaced by a new and loftier aspiration never before considered or contemplated.

Several years ago, I wrote a book entitled *A Christmas Snow* that was subsequently made into a movie with the same title. After the success of that movie, it was made into a musical stage play that ran for over 100 performances. Veteran actor Muse Watson of *NCIS* fame played the lead role in both the movie and musical stage play. I remember talking with Muse during a particularly frustrating day of rehearsals shortly before opening night. Everyone in the cast and crew seemed to be panicking about all the things that needed to be done and tasks that had to be completed before the opening.

At the height of the chaos, Muse turned to me, and in that resonant, famous voice, said, "Jim, at times like this, I try to remember how well things in life turn out for me when I just do the next thing right, and do the right thing next." Muse's statement was uttered in a moment and remains profound for a lifetime.

As you go through your day today, remember beginnings and endings come and go, and *today's the day!*

The Rear View Mirror

You may have heard someone say referring to a particu-larly frustrating or embarrassing moment, "If I had only known then what I know now..." You may have even said or felt this yourself. While it would be nice to be able to relive our past with the benefit of our current wisdom and knowledge, this is impossible. You can't avoid a bad situation with wisdom you gained from the bad situation you are trying to avoid.

William Blake said, "You must live your life going forward, but you can only understand it looking backward." This leaves us with the prospect of boldly moving ahead into uncharted waters without any personal experience or understanding of many situations; however, we need not move into the future unarmed. A smart person learns from his or her own mistakes, while a wise person learns from the mistakes and experiences of others.

Virtually everyone is going through their daily lives hoping to have a great idea. The only thing you need to do to have a great idea is wait for something bad to happen in your daily routine and ask the pertinent question, "How could I have avoided that?" The answer to that simple question is a great idea. Taking it one step further, you can simply ask, "How can I help other people avoid that?" The answer to that question introduces a great opportunity, venture, or business.

You need not experience every problem or challenge in life to learn from it. When you're driving along a road that you think is only wet but you see that a car in front of you has slid into the ditch, you can gain wisdom from their experience by realizing the road is not merely wet but covered with black ice; you can, therefore, reduce your speed, proceed with caution, and avoid a situation revealed by someone else. Life is navigated looking through the windshield but understood peering into the rear view mirror.

You can meet the wisest people who ever lived and learn their profound secrets gained through their own mistakes, errors, and painful experiences within the pages of many great biographies. Always think before you act, and if you don't have any personal experience to consider, study the path that others have traveled before you, and avoid the pitfalls.

As you go through your day today, keep your windshield clean and your rearview mirror focused.

Today's the day!

PAYING PROMPTLY
PAYS DIVIDENDS

I AM NOT LIKE MANY AUTHORS, SPEAKERS, OR COLUMNISTS who share theories or talk about their past success. I run a business with several different divisions on a daily basis. The ideas and concepts in these weekly columns come out of my own real-life experiences.

Primarily due to my blindness, I like to work with a very small, highly-skilled and talented team. People who read about or come to learn of our business involving a television network, 30 books, six movies, ongoing arena speeches around the world, as well as the weekly columns might assume there are dozens or even hundreds of people who work here. In reality, there are six of us.

Many reporters, analysts, and observers upon learning this ask incredulously, "Why do you work with six people?" The answer is I haven't discovered how to do all that we do with five people.

Entrepreneurs who value or calibrate the size of a business based on the number of employees are making a huge mistake. There are companies with thousands of employees that are losing money at an unbelievable rate; and on the other hand, there are very efficient, organized entrepreneurs who work by themselves with a few strategic contractors or vendors who earn incredible profits.

Since I can't read print or do paperwork, I strive to deal with any files, correspondence, or printed material only once; therefore, when the mail comes in each day, I answer it immediately, including approving the bills and having them paid that day. Initially, I pursued this practice as a way to simplify my life and make my workday more efficient; however, over the years, I have discovered that paying the bills the day they come in offers several other benefits.

Please understand I am well aware of the accounting and business principles surrounding having accounts payable and delaying the payments to the last conceivable moment. Given current low interest rates, there are often very few economic reasons to delay or withhold a payment. On the other hand, though it was not my original intent, I have become legendary with my vendors, contractors, and those people with whom I do business in my industry. I am told by these individuals that they receive my check weeks or even months before they receive checks from any other customers or contractors in that payment cycle.

Imagine you are one of these individuals who work for a major corporation within the TV, book publishing, movie, event, newspaper, or magazine industry, and you have to determine whose call to return promptly, whose favor you choose to grant, or whose proposal you decide to give first and full consideration. My competitors often wonder why my firm gets treated differently. It's simply because we treat everyone else differently.

As you go through your day today, remember the Golden Rule always works even when paying your bills.

Today's the day!

A Critical Look at Critics

ANYONE WHO SUCCEEDS IN OUR WORLD TODAY HAS TO UNDER-
stand and manage the role of criticism. Criticism ranges from
very constructive to maliciously destructive.

To my knowledge, there has never been a monument erected
to a critic. Most critics are self-proclaimed and have no more
knowledge of what they are criticizing than the general public,
and often they have less knowledge and questionable motives.

Four of my novels have been turned into major motion pic-
tures with two more in production. In the movie business, we
live and die on the success of the opening weekend box office
numbers in theaters across the country and around the world.
These box office numbers can be greatly impacted by movie
critics. I often remind myself that movies such as *The Wizard of
Oz*, *Star Wars*, and *Gone with the Wind* were viciously attacked
by the critics of the day. While we think of these films today as
monumental and groundbreaking, the movie critics who first
saw those tremendous theatrical accomplishments failed to see
the screen treasures that time and the judgment of the public
have revealed.

While it's likely you do not make your living in the book or movie business, you, nevertheless, deal with critics in your life and your profession. When you receive any criticism, it is important, first, to examine the motives and the bias of the critic. Critics are seeking approval of their own work and often get more notoriety for tearing someone down than for building them up. After you explore the critic's motives, you must honestly and objectively measure whether or not the criticism is valid.

It is difficult to take a step back from our work and see it for what it truly is in the harsh light of day. Most great improvement comes from the reaction to constructive, well-placed criticism. It is important to differentiate between your critics and your customers.

You can't succeed in the movie industry by selling tickets to movie critics. Audiences usually have a mind of their own. If you want a truly valid and objective opinion of your work, ask those whom you serve, not those who go out of their way to criticize you.

The Internet and online feedback sites have made it quick and easy for anyone to give their personal thumbs up or thumbs down on virtually anything from a restaurant meal to a hotel room to a book or movie. These unsolicited remarks from real consumers mean far more to you and me than the ramblings of a self-proclaimed critic.

As you go through your day today, use the power of criticism to succeed.

Today's the day!

MAKING THE RIGHT TURN

MOST CHANGE AND IMPROVEMENT COMES IN SMALL STEPS AND minute increments. I grow tired of politicians, critics, and commentators who respond to good ideas by proclaiming, "That suggestion won't solve the entire problem."

I have a friend and colleague who is a well-known author and speaker. He is fond of explaining, "One hundred 1 percent solutions are as good as a 100 percent solution." Long-term success rarely comes from the grand-slam homerun or the 100-yard touchdown run. It, instead, comes from moving the runner to first base or the football down the field.

Recently I read about an amazing breakthrough improvement made by United Parcel Service. UPS saved over $25 million in a decade, delivered more packages in a shorter time, and improved safety while lowering their carbon emissions impact by simply routing their trucks to cut out left-hand turns. An enterprising person at UPS discovered that by using the computer to establish more efficient routes that incorporated a series of right-hand looping turns instead of left-hand turns which force drivers to cross traffic and wait for lights to change, the company cut costs, improved safety, and increased profits.

Now I can hear the gloom-and-doom critics whining, "What does $25 million over 10 years really mean to UPS?" Any time you run across someone who thinks $25 million doesn't matter, just tell them to make that check out to Jim Stovall, and they can reach me via the contact information provided at the back of the book.

The breakthrough in the right-hand turn policy is not just the $25 million, the improved efficiency, the increased safety, or the lowered emissions—it fosters a culture of thought, exploration, and improvement. If you can get a group of people to stop criticizing every thought or idea that doesn't solve the whole problem, and get them to start looking for 1 percent improvements in their own sphere of influence or scope of work, you can change the world.

Great ideas build upon one another. They come about when average people think and act in extraordinary ways.

As you go through your day today, look for the 1 percent right turn in your own world.

Today's the day!

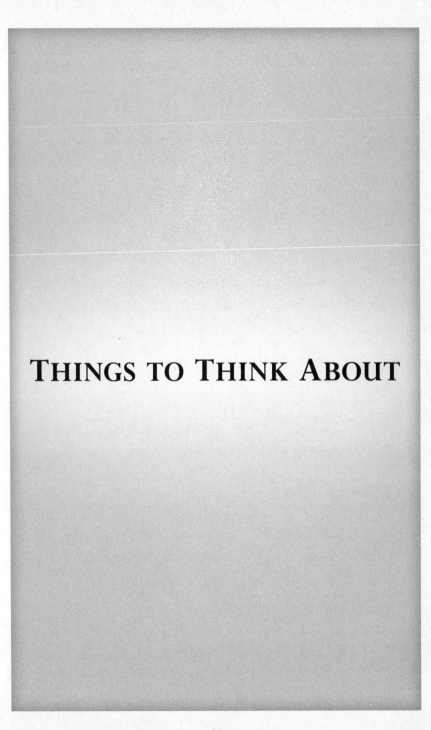

THINGS TO THINK ABOUT

FINANCIAL PLANNING
FOR THE BIRDS

BIRDS ARE AMONG THE MOST FASCINATING CREATURES ON earth. Bird watching is one of the most popular hobbies. I believe people enjoy watching birds because birds have mastered the art of flight. Most birds are able to fly, but they do it in different ways.

Birds are able to propel themselves through thin air by using three different methods of flight. Most birds achieve flight by flapping their wings. This great effort on their part causes them to have enough momentum so that the air flowing under their wings creates lift. Some birds, after they have flapped their wings for a period of time, are able to glide. They can, in essence, coast using the momentum they have previously generated by flapping their wings. The most elite performers and the rarest in the bird world are able to soar. These enlightened creatures, through understanding air currents and thermals, are able to use the environment around them and their understanding of it to fly for hours and many miles with very little or no effort on their own part.

When it comes to money, we can all learn from our friends the birds.

Most people among us know no way to survive financially other than flapping their wings through working at a job and living paycheck-to-paycheck. These people work hard and spend every penny they earn—and often a bit more—thanks to our culture of credit.

Then there are the individuals who have flapped their financial wings long enough to save a few dollars so they can glide for a relatively brief period of time on the income that their previous effort has brought them. While this is better than frantically flapping through your entire financial life, there is still a far better way to travel.

There are a few elite financial birds among us who have mastered the art of soaring. They started out by working hard for their money while they were learning how to make their money work hard for them. These successful financial flyers can use the financial environment around them via interest, dividends, and capital gains much like the eagles use wind currents and thermals to reach heights others cannot even imagine.

The next time you decide to go bird watching, don't forget the financial lessons our feathered friends can teach us.

As you go through your day today, commit to soaring financially like the eagles.

Today's the day!

THE LACK OF LOTTERY LOGIC

THERE ARE FEW IDEAS MORE INTERESTING OR THOUGHTS MORE compelling than instant wealth. Becoming an overnight millionaire and going from rags to riches is the unfulfilled dream of most people.

If you are a regular reader of Winners' Wisdom columns, you have observed me picking on the lottery and casinos before. My argument is not as much moral and ethical as it is an argument of finances and focus. I have no real objection to someone who wants to buy an occasional lottery ticket for entertainment purposes as long as they are out of debt, and the lottery ticket money doesn't take food off the family table. I've never found anything particularly entertaining, myself, about spending hard-earned money on the immensely overwhelming probability of losing, but if others find pleasure in it, it's okay with me.

My objection is to the millions of people around the world who spend money their family cannot afford to lose on lottery tickets. This destroys people, potential, and possibilities in several ways. If the average person who consistently plays the lottery and buys tickets in amounts that equal the national average would simply invest the same amount of money each week in an average growth-stock mutual fund, they would be millionaires within 20 years. So it's not just the loss of the money spent on losing tickets. It's the loss of the potential they are flushing away a few dollars at a time.

David J. Hand, author of *The Improbability Principle*, says, "1,167,843 years (or 15 thousand lifetimes) is how long you'd have to play Powerball to have a 50/50 chance of winning a jackpot." I believe your hard-earned money, your family's future, and all of your hopes and dreams deserve better odds than this.

The idea of getting rich quick is a pipedream that robs your resources and your possibilities. Creating a wealth plan provides a certainty over time of financial freedom and success.

The index of the entire stock market has averaged nearly 12 percent compounded over the last half of a century, while the lottery requires you to throw away your hard-earned money consistently for more than a million years for an even chance of winning. If the logic and numbers don't make it clear to you, stay tuned, because I'm sure I will write about it again as I know the casinos and lotteries are going to continue to share their propaganda.

As you go through your day today, invest logically, and get the odds in your favor.

Today's the day!

MEDIA MYTHS

AS SOMEONE WHO ENJOYED PLAYING FOOTBALL MYSELF AND AS a lifelong fan of the game, I have been distressed at the recent media coverage chronicling the domestic violence, substance abuse, and other criminal activities of players in the National Football League. Please understand, one instance of domestic violence, child abuse, or any other crime is too many, whether it's an NFL player or you and me.

I remain hopeful that the intense media coverage will not only prompt change in the NFL, but more importantly, in our society as a whole.

This morning, as is my habit, I listened to the satellite radio reports from *The Wall Street Journal*. Today they did a story that was first reported by *Forbes* that totally astounded me. I was prompted to check and recheck the facts before I shared them with you. According to *Forbes*, as reported by *The Wall Street Journal*, the average man in his late 20s is about nine times more likely to be arrested than an NFL player for any cause.

Football players are more likely to be involved in a violent crime when they are arrested, but they are still less likely to be involved in domestic abuse or other violent incidences than the general public.

I'm very hopeful that the NFL will take appropriate steps to clean up its own house and improve upon what is already a lower incidence of domestic violence and crime than the general public; however, there are two very important lessons to be learned for you and me. First, violence is not a desirable response or a solution to problems. Second, the media has the ability and willingness to magnify anything far beyond its normal proportion.

While there are definitely improvements that need to be made in the NFL and among active players, we must not get so busy pointing our fingers at these high-profile individuals that we forget to look in the mirror at our own communities, families, and ourselves.

Even when the media is fair and accurate, the intense nature of the spotlight that they bring to bear causes every situation to be blown out of proportion. The media can serve as a great indicator of society's direction, but it rarely gives us an accurate measure of the real world in which we all live.

As you go through your day today, learn the true lessons that the media can teach us all.

Today's the day!

My Thanks to You

My dear reader, as my weekly column concluded its fifteenth year appearing in newspapers, magazines, and online publications around the world, I found myself both grateful and humble.

A new hardcover book made up of a compilation of these weekly columns was released by The Napoleon Hill Foundation entitled *Wisdom for Winners*. A 5-star book review appeared in *Success* magazine.

I realize some have read the more than 800 columns I have written in the past decade-and-a-half while others are just joining this growing worldwide community of *Winners' Wisdom* readers, but I appreciate each and every one of you.

There have been many messages in the 30 books I have written as well as in the four major motion pictures based on my novels, but the most enduring and widely accepted message may be that of the Golden List. The Golden List is a concept and a daily routine I learned from my grandmother. Apparently on one particular day as a preschool child, I was expressing my dissatisfaction with the current state of affairs. My grandmother told me, "You can whine and complain all you want just as soon as you finish your Golden List." When I inquired what The Golden List was, she told me that we needed to sit down and make a list of ten things I was thankful for today, and then I would be free to complain and criticize until my heart was content.

I found on that fateful day and am reminded each morning of my life a half-century later that it is impossible to focus on things for which you are thankful and still have a bad day.

I'm in the habit of getting up at 4:00 a.m. each day to do much of my reading, studying, and planning before heading to the office, TV studio, or speaking engagement where I will be working; but before anything else happens, I conclude my Golden List of things for which I am grateful.

The Golden List became a bit of a worldwide phenomenon when I wrote about it in my book *The Ultimate Gift* which was turned into a major motion picture from Twentieth Century Fox. It is hard for me to go anywhere without having people tell me what the Golden List has meant to them, their family, and their colleagues. While I am grateful that the Golden List has meant so much to so many other people, the biggest bene-ficiary of the Golden List may well be me.

Yesterday, as my colleagues read to me the advanced copy of the book review that will appear in *Success* magazine, I found myself being thankful for Don Green and everyone at The Napoleon Hill Foundation, Dave Wildasin and his team at my publisher Sound Wisdom, and my colleagues here in my office. But even more than these wonderful colleagues and friends, I found myself being immensely grateful for you, because as you conclude reading this column, you have once again honored me and made it possible for my dream to come true.

As you go through your day today, think of all the things for which you are thankful, and remember, I am thankful for you.

Today's the day!

THOUGHTS, ACTIONS, AND RESULTS

AMONG LIFE'S MOST ENDURING PRINCIPLES IS THE FACT THAT we become what we think about. This was the motivation for my latest book. *Poems, Quotes, and Things to Think About* gives readers bite-sized thoughts that can shape their day, hour, or even the next moment. (Visit: http://ow.ly/E4ixg.)

Recently in the field of success and personal development, there has been a school of thought that has emerged claiming that our thoughts can bring things into reality. While this is true, there is generally a step in-between thoughts and results. This step is action, our own efforts required to turn our thoughts into results.

Too many people have taken this teaching to heart as they sit on their couch watching a DVD or reading a book as they await what they believe will be their inevitable success. Our thoughts rarely change results directly. Instead, our thoughts change us, then we act, bringing on the results we desire.

If someone claims to believe something, but they do not act upon it, I question their belief.

I am sitting in my office as I dictate the words for this column. If someone rushed in and shouted, "The building's on fire!" but I just continued to just sit here dictating, they would wonder whether I heard their warning and if I believe them or not. If I told them that I did hear them and believe them but continued to sit here, taking no action, there is an obvious disconnect. The warning of the fire is intended to change my thoughts, eliciting an action such as exiting the building, which would bring the desired result of saving my life.

Simply understanding there is a fire and even thinking about the fire without action cannot bring a positive result. In this case, it could bring a very deadly result.

Shakespeare said that our eyes are the windows to our soul. I believe that our actions provide a window or a clue to our thoughts. No matter what someone tells you they know, think, or believe, their actions will always give them away. People can claim to be serious about their goals and committed to the results, but if you simply examine their checkbook and their calendar, the reality will be clear.

How we spend our time and how we spend our money reveal our thoughts and the underlying priorities. I hope you will take control of your thoughts to an extent where they take control of your actions and provide the results you desire. You may be able to fool your friends, your family, and even the whole world, but you'll never fool your thoughts.

As you go through your day today, master your thoughts and sample *Poems, Quotes, and Things to Think About.*

Today's the day!

Stumbling to Success

I'VE HEARD IT SAID THAT SUCCESS IS A MATTER OF AVOIDING mistakes. While this seems like good advice, it's not strictly accurate. Successful people make their share of mistakes. They simply manage them.

I believe that a fool makes the same mistake over and over while a wise person makes a new mistake every day.

The goal should be to learn from every mistake not necessarily to avoid them. The best way to learn from a mistake is to learn from someone else's mistake. If you observe world-class golfers in championship tournaments, you will see them squat down behind their ball as it is sitting on the green so they can judge the undulations and breaks of the surface between their golf ball and the hole. Really great golfers not only observe the greens surrounding their own shots, but they observe their opponent's ball as it rolls toward the hole. This is called "going to school" on your opponent. If the green has an unexpected break, causing a putt to curve one way or the other more than expected, it is far better to learn from your opponent's shot than from your own.

All of us make mistakes. Unsuccessful people call this failure while successful people call it fertilizer. It may not be pleasant at the time, but it can help your dreams grow into reality in the future.

Great ideas are generally inspired by mistakes, challenges, or problems. If you go through your daily routine and wait for something bad to happen, you have the potential of a great idea. As cited previously, all you need to do is ask yourself the critical question, "How could I have avoided that?" The answer to that question is a great idea. All you have to do to have a great business is ask yourself one further question, "How could I help other people avoid that?" The answer to this second question is a great business opportunity.

The world will give you fame, fortune, and acclaim if you simply recognize and solve other people's problems.

Mistakes are part of the human condition. Maturity comes when we learn from our mistakes and resolve to not repeat them. I have always appreciated the great line sung by Billy Joel. "I am the entertainer. I had to pay my price. The things I did not know at first, I learned by doing twice." The great lessons of life come to us disguised as problems, challenges, and mistakes.

As you go through your day today, learn from each mistake, and don't repeat it.

Today's the day!

HUMANS AND BEING

A MAN FOR ALL SEASONS

I RECEIVED THE SAD BUT NOT UNEXPECTED NEWS THAT ONE OF my friends, teachers, and mentors had passed away. I met John when I was still a teenager and beginning college. He was around 50 years of age at that time and was already a successful and well-respected person in our community. Nevertheless, John befriended me, and we began a business and personal relationship that lasted for several decades.

John shared many great lessons with me and taught me the power of reading personal development books and biographies, but more important than what he said was what he did. His actions spoke for themselves. Over the ensuing years—thanks to movies, books, television, arena events, and my weekly columns—my success and notoriety grew. This created a strain in some of my friendships but never with John. He was my biggest fan and cheerleader while helping to keep me grounded in the past while focused on the future.

I visited John in the hospital one weekend, which inevitably turned out to be our last time together. It was a sad but poignant time. I left the next day for a speaking engagement on the West Coast followed by two others that week. During my travels, I got the word that John had passed away.

His family asked me to speak at his memorial service, which was an honor I treasured; but then I discovered that John's service was scheduled during my third speaking engagement that week. Ironically, I was scheduled to be onstage bringing a message of possibility and hope at the very hour of my friend John's memorial service.

I was facing a quandary as I have not yet mastered the feat of being in two places at the same time. As I was wrestling with the decision to speak at John's service or the convention where I was contracted to be, I thought about the years with John and the lessons he had taught me including: always do what you say, do your best, and focus on the future. Although I was conflicted in my grief, when I thought about the lessons John had taught me, I knew exactly what he would have me do.

At the appointed hour, I walked onto a stage and delivered a 90-minute speech just as I had agreed to do; however, that speech was a bit different from any I had done before or any I will ever do again in that it was a tribute to my friend John on the day and hour of his memorial service. I introduced my audience to my friend through the lessons he had taught and the life he had lived. The only real tribute we can give to those who have gone before us is to keep their legacy alive and pass it on.

As you go through your day today, live out the lessons your heroes and mentors gave you.

Today's the day!

FROM BUFFETT TO BUFFETT

AT FIRST GLANCE, THERE WOULD SEEM TO BE NO MORE OPPO-
site people than Warren Buffett and Jimmy Buffett. For years,
there has been speculation about how they might be related. It
would appear that any family tie would have to be many gen-
erations into the past.

Warren Buffett seems to be the button-down, num-
ber-crunching, Wall Street wizard while Jimmy Buffett seems
to be the happy-go-lucky, barefoot, beach-party-forever guy. In
reality, Warren Buffett creates money while having fun, and
Jimmy Buffett creates fun while making money. We can learn
from both of these gentlemen.

Warren Buffett has accumulated unprecedented wealth by
generating amazing investment returns over many decades.
While he is respected for his wisdom and insight, he is admired
for his down-home lifestyle in Omaha where he enjoys the fruits
of the companies he owns such as Coca-Cola, Dairy Queen,
and others. Stockholders' meetings generally hold all of the
entertainment value of watching paint dry or grass grow, but
Warren Buffett's Berkshire Hathaway stockholders' meetings
have been described as the Woodstock for capitalists. Warren

Buffet's stockholders' meetings involve singing, dancing, and serenades with Warren himself playing the ukulele.

Many people think Jimmy Buffett retired decades ago after his big hit *Margaritaville*. Nothing could be further from the truth as he tours constantly each summer selling out stadiums across the country and, literally, around the world. Jimmy Buffett has a group of fanatical followers known as Parrotheads. Parrotheads party with vigor but also have a conscience. There are Parrothead chapters across the country that have sprung up somewhat independent from Jimmy Buffett while following the messages in his music. These Parrothead chapters have raised millions of dollars for local charities and international environmental causes. When you look at Jimmy Buffett's business empire including restaurants, clubs, casinos, concerts, recording, and much more, you see the connection between fun and finance that is the hallmark of both Jimmy Buffett and Warren Buffett.

The late, great entertainer George Burns who performed right up until his death at almost 100 years of age, often said, "If you love what you do, you never work a day in your life." I believe both Buffetts have found a way to do this. They have found a way to both work hard and play hard all at the same time.

As you go through your day today, pursue profit and passion in the same place.

Today's the day!

CAUSE AND EFFECT

THERE IS AN AGE-OLD DEBATE AS TO WHETHER WE SING BECAUSE we're happy, or we're happy because we sing. This is the proverbial chicken-and-egg discussion that has no real resolution.

Shakespeare said that our face is like a book that reveals what we are feeling. Charles Darwin said our faces can actually affect or impact our feelings. I believe both Shakespeare and Darwin were right.

I have the opportunity to mentor and counsel many executives and entrepreneurs around the world. Invariably, their success comes down to doing something at some point that they don't want to do. I always encourage these individuals to act as if they wanted to do the thing they are avoiding, and before long, they will find they are enjoying it. The dreaded task can actually become a point of happiness and joy in their lives.

My late, great friend and mentor Zig Ziglar found himself overweight and out of shape at one point in his life and undertook a regimen of jogging every day. The first day, Zig ran once around his block and collapsed in his front yard with exhaustion. The next day, he reported making it one block and one mailbox, collapsing in his neighbor's yard. He progressed a mailbox-a-day until he could make it twice around the block, then three times, then even more. Eventually Zig was running several miles each day at a very competitive pace.

I heard Zig tell about his persistent efforts many times from the stage. He would get this pained tone in his voice proclaiming, "You've got to pay the price for success." Then one day, Zig told me he had been jogging early in the morning along the coast near an arena where he would be speaking that afternoon. As he described it, the sun was shining, the temperature was perfect, the birds were singing, and there were a number of other runners along his path, most of whom were younger and were quickly passed by an enthusiastic Zig Ziglar.

Suddenly, it dawned on him that he wasn't paying the price for success. He was enjoying the price of success, and if he hadn't put in the effort, he would be paying the price for failure.

Our actions create our emotions, and our emotions create our actions. Whether the chicken or the egg came first, if we will just feed our chickens and gather our eggs, we will succeed.

As you go through your day today, do the thing you enjoy, and enjoy the thing you do.

Today's the day!

GOING TO THE WELL

IT'S BEEN SAID THAT LEADERS ARE READERS, AND READERS ARE
leaders. This is true as the most common characteristic
among top executives and millionaire entrepreneurs is the
fact that they consistently read instructional, inspirational, or
motivational books.

Throughout the years, there have been many great suc-
cess-oriented authors. Many of them will quote successful
people they have known or read about from the past. If you
read enough of these books, you will experience an author
quoting a previous author, who is also quoting a previous
author, who is also referring to something he read, that was
originally said by an historical or successful individual. While
it's good to read what other people think about someone else's
feelings regarding another person's perspective, I believe if
you want the pure water, you've got to go to the well.

I believe the greatest success writer of the last century
would probably be Napoleon Hill, and the greatest orator
may well have been Winston Churchill. While I enjoy read-
ing other people quoting these giants, I always try to get back
to the well periodically and read Napoleon Hill and listen to

Winston Churchill. Somehow, when others are trying to use these legends as an example or something to build upon, they often inadvertently dilute the meaning or power.

These original thinkers along with many others broke new ground in what they wrote and said. Others may have built upon their work, including myself, but I hope whenever you read these luminaries referred to, it will prompt you to pick up a book or recording and go back to the original source.

Napoleon Hill wrote: "Every adversity, every failure, every heartache carries with it the seed of an equal or greater benefit." It is significant to understand that Hill developed and wrote these thoughts during the Great Depression. There was little to be optimistic about, but his words caused people then and now to begin looking for a brighter day and a new beginning in the midst of every problem.

Winston Churchill said, "Never give in. Never give in. Never, never, never, never—in nothing, great or small, large or petty—never give in, except to convictions of honour and good sense." These thoughts were formed in the great leader's mind during the depths of World War II at a time when it looked like the British Empire could be wiped from the face of the earth, and the only reasonable course of action might be to surrender.

One of my favorite authors, Louis L'Amour, often said, "A man can only be judged against the backdrop of the time and place in which he lived."

I hope this will prompt you to go back and review a bit of Napoleon Hill, Winston Churchill, and even Louis L'Amour.

As you go through your day today, enjoy the commentators and educators, but always go back to the well.

Today's the day!

Enjoying Today and Tomorrow

IN MY BOOK *THE MILLIONAIRE MAP*, I OFFERED MY READERS around the world the opportunity to take a free online millionaire assessment. This assessment reveals thoughts, ideas, and long-held beliefs that may keep an individual from reaching their goals or help them succeed. If you would like to take this assessment, just go to www.TheMillionaireMap.com.

Even though *The Millionaire Map* book topped one of the best-seller lists and we have received a flood of millionaire profiles, I have been able, to date, to respond to each of them personally. There have been many revelations that people have shared with me from their past financial successes and failures. One gentleman was describing the attitudes and behaviors that had drug him into bankruptcy as he declared, "We got lost in the world of indulgence and then got lost in the world of regret." This poignant phrase, borne out of one family's pain, can teach us all many things.

Regret is an emotion that can be used to measure immediate and delayed gratification. A balanced life contains both immediate and delayed gratification, but the extent and degree must be weighed against regret. There are activities we do not enjoy now but will result in much joy later. Conversely, there are activities we might enjoy today but we will regret in the future.

As we look at our health, wealth, personal, or professional lives, we must always balance the immediate and the eventual. Some people save everything for a rainy day. Much of life can pass them by, and many fruits of their labor can spoil while avoiding a rain that never comes. On the other hand, it is much more common in our world today to see people who use up all they have and everything they can borrow today with a total disregard for tomorrow.

One of the greatest preschool tests of future success involves putting a young child in a room and giving them one cookie. The child is told, "You can eat the cookie now or wait a few minutes, and I will come back and give you a second cookie if you don't eat this one before then." The preschoolers who wait for the second cookie grow up to understand the value of higher education, compound interest, long-term dividends, and lifelong relationships. The young person who eats their cookie immediately often goes through life the same way, experiencing nothing-down loans, buy-now-pay-later deals, dropouts, layoffs, and revolving superficial relationships.

We must live our lives to maximize joy and minimize regrets.

As you go through your day today, do the thing that will make you happy now and later.

Today's the day!

PATIENCE AND PROCRASTINATION

PATIENCE IS A SIGNIFICANT ELEMENT OF SUCCESS, AND PRO-crastination is a significant element of failure.

To an outside observer, patience and procrastination can look the same. The difference between patience and procrastination can be determined by whether you're waiting on something or something is waiting on you.

If you drive by a farm during the springtime and there appears to be no activity underway, it may be because the farmer has already planted and is patiently waiting for the next phase of his activity; or it could mean the farmer is procrastinating and avoiding the task of planting, which could endanger or ruin his crop.

I meet many aspiring entrepreneurs at speaking engagements, movie premieres, and book signings. When I inquire about their current project or next opportunity, they will often use platitudes such as, "I'm waiting for my ship to come in," or "I'm waiting to get all my ducks in a row." In reality, they never sent a ship out, and they've been waiting so long, their pier collapsed; and not only are their ducks not in a row, but they flew off or died of old age a long time ago.

If you have a dream, a goal, or an ambition, it requires some activity today. I have written almost 1,000 weekly columns that are read by countless people around the world in newspapers, magazines, and online publications. I hope each column contains some useful advice or powerful principle, but without exception, every column—including this one—ends with the phrase "Today's the day!"

It doesn't matter what you know now if you don't do something today. Maybe it's only a matter of studying something or meeting a key person, but you need to be doing something today. There will be days when your activity will involve patiently waiting for something you have done to develop or emerge into reality.

If you have called an influential person to make a key contact, you may be patiently waiting for the person to call you back; or you may be afraid to make the call, so you are simply procrastinating. Patience is productive. Procrastination is useless.

Patience involves celebrating the task you have done while waiting for the seed you have planted to grow. Procrastination involves avoiding what you know needs to be done, which makes a mockery of your passion, your goals, and your destiny.

As you go through your day today, utilize patience and reject procrastination.

Today's the day!

Maximizing Your Mind

We use our minds to try to understand how everything in the world works, but the subject we may know least about is our mind itself. Scientists have determined that the thing our minds may be most effective at doing is misleading, fooling, or deluding us. Whether it's the airline pilot on approach who doesn't see a jumbo jet sitting right in front of him on the runway because he doesn't expect to, or the multitude of eyewitnesses who each emphatically report they all saw something different from one another, it's clear that our minds are complicated entities that are part of us and somewhat independent agents at the same time.

The more we learn about how our minds work, the more it is clear that we are just beginning to scratch the surface of how we think, how we process, how we remember, and how we learn.

Much of the study about the human mind centers on academic pursuits, but there are a few recent breakthroughs that can be very practical to you and me in our personal and professional lives.

Recently it has been determined that making a decision is one of the most difficult tasks our minds perform. The decision-making process takes a tremendous amount of energy whether the decision we are making is a significant one or not. Science has revealed that the fewer decisions people make, the more rational they are in the decision-making process. It seems that high-functioning minds are engaged primarily in high-functioning problems.

Many great leaders and thinkers historically ate the same thing for breakfast, traveled the same way to work or school, and wore the same clothes on a regular basis. Routine decisions for many high-functioning thinkers are more a matter of habit than thought.

While great thinkers use their minds in conjunction with the latest technology in processing problems and solutions, they are likely to utilize notecards or a tablet of paper to keep their daily "to do" list.

While multitasking has become popular, it is not as efficient as we may think. Our minds seem to measure our progress based on how busy we feel or how stressed we are mentally; therefore, doing several things at once may give us a feeling of great achievement. In reality, when progress is measured, we could be better off by focusing on one thing at a time.

While our minds might tell us the longer and harder we focus the better we will perform, in reality research has shown that working in two-hour blocks of time, punctuated by a break or even a nap, may provide better results.

Data has shown that the highest-functioning, most-efficient minds may well be the least-distracted minds. Controlling email, phone calls, and other interruptions gives our minds the best chance to do their greatest work.

We are all different and function best in a variety of ways, but before you determine how you function most efficiently, it would be wise to measure your results instead of trusting how you feel.

As you go through your day today, remember that your mind is a powerful tool. Use it well.

Today's the day!

CHANGING OURSELVES

WE HAVE ALL HEARD THE WISE SAYING, "THE ONLY CONSTANT in the world is change." Change is, indeed, inevitable and has always been part of human existence, but the pace of change seems to be accelerating. Change is uncomfortable for us all. If we are honest with ourselves, we will admit we have a bias toward the way things are in our world today.

In addition to writing columns, I also write books, make speeches, produce movies, and run a television network. As part of my duties as president of the Narrative Television Network, several years ago I was called upon to make a presentation at a city council meeting in Houston since we were negotiating for channel space on the various cable TV systems there.

When I arrived at the city council meeting, I was informed that our presentation was the second one on the agenda, and the first presentation would be a proposal to install a light rail system throughout the Houston area. The promoter of the rail system explained to the city council and the rest of us assembled there that a commuter train system would relieve the overburdened surface street and expressway system throughout Houston and help with the endless traffic jams they were experiencing. When one of the city councilors asked if there were any polling results showing people's preference to ride the train, the promoter of the light rail system responded, "No one wants to ride the train. They just want everyone else to ride the train so they can continue to drive to work the way they have always done."

At the end of the day, we thankfully got our channel on the Houston cable TV system, and the light rail commuter train system proposal was rejected; but the enduring lesson I learned from that meeting was the fact that the only change we eagerly embrace is the change that will cause other people to alter their activities so we can keep ours the same.

While we should never change simply for the sake of being different, we must be willing to keep an open mind and try to focus upon what we want to get done and not how we want to do it. We must keep our mission as a permanent fixture and constant while being flexible enough with our methods to allow for change.

My late, great friend and colleague Paul Harvey was fond of saying, "Not everything we call progress is progress." Just because it's different, it's not automatically better, but it's not inevitably worse.

As you go through your day today, don't focus on change or staying the same. Focus on being the best.

Today's the day!

QUANTUM LEAPS

TOOLS AND TALENT

HERE IN THE 21ST CENTURY IT IS EASY TO TAKE THE MARVELS OF the computer age for granted. Things that seem commonplace to us now would have been science fiction a decade ago and complete fantasy a generation ago.

Many of us have deep-seated dreams and aspirations to create our masterpiece as a legacy of our life and time here on earth. It's normal to want to leave something of ourselves behind so that when we are gone we will not be forgotten. When we think of the masters such as Mozart, Shakespeare, Mark Twain, or Ernest Hemingway, we often look at their work and forget the tools with which they created their enduring masterpieces. The most basic Smart Phone or iPad would have been an unimaginable quantum leap to any of these geniuses.

As I dictate the words that are being typed into a computer for this column, it is easy to forget that the ability to edit with ease, check spelling and punctuation, or instantly translate into dozens of languages is a recent phenomenon. If Shakespeare had only had the most basic word processing software, or Beethoven had had the benefit of simple editing and mixing technology that is available on your hand-held device, one shudders to think how much more output would have been generated from their life's work. Maybe they would have grown complacent with the technology as we too often do, but I tend to think the masters would have harnessed the potential of these modern-day miracles.

The critical component in creating your masterpiece remains the unparalleled computerized graphic generator that is housed between your ears. The best programs and technology we have today to enhance our creativity are little more than a blank slate until we accept the task of filling in the blanks. Mozart still had to play and write the first note, and Shakespeare still had to imagine the first scene of one of his plays and the first line from the first character. The barriers to creativity and moats around our masterpieces are still our own lack of willingness to engage in the task.

One of my favorite 20th century authors, James Michener, was fond of saying, "The average aspiring writer is filled with seven volumes of garbage that they are, unfortunately, not willing to write through to get to the treasure beneath." As in most things in life, greatness begins when you begin.

My late, great friend and mentor Dr. Robert Schuller often said, "Starting is halfway there." Most people don't fail to achieve. They fail to begin.

As you go through your day today, honor the masters and begin your masterpiece.

Today's the day!

THE FAILURE FORMULA

I OFTEN THINK THAT FAILURE IS THE MOST MISUNDERSTOOD element of the human condition. Failure is not the opposite of success. Failure is, instead, part of success.

Every great invention, accomplishment, or victory is preceded by a failure or, in most cases, a series of failures. When we understand that failure is part of the success process, we then come to understand that as long as we don't quit, failure is not final. It is simply fertilizer for future success.

I am a huge baseball fan and enjoy listening to the satellite radio broadcasts of games most every night during the baseball season. My father was, for a brief time, a Minor League baseball player, and he had the distinction of playing in a game against Mickey Mantle. This always inspired me to play and enjoy baseball. Today, as a totally blind person, I am absolutely convinced and could guarantee you that I can get a hit off of the best pitcher in the Major Leagues if you will allow me to take as many strikes as I want. As long as I keep swinging, I know that sooner or later I'm going to hit the ball and reach my goal.

We live in a microwave world, but success remains a crockpot proposition. We see great athletes performing on television in multiple slow-motion replays. What we don't see are the thousands of failures that came before the success. We don't see the stumbles and falls followed by those athletes picking themselves up, brushing themselves off, and trying again. When you only experience the gold medal competition and the victor being crowned, you miss the true essence of success, which is pushing through repeated failures.

Recent research has shown that to become a world-class master of any art or task, one must practice for 10,000 hours. Most of these 10,000 hours of practice involve immediate failure, identifying mistakes, recommitting our efforts, and trying again.

In any cross-country flight, pilots tell me that the plane is off course the vast majority of the time. After the pilot takes off and checks the heading, discovering that they have veered from their intended heading, they don't turn around, go back to the airport where they started, land the plane, and declare the flight a failure. They simply make the necessary adjustments and get the plane back on course. In this way, a successful landing follows hundreds of slight failures and course corrections that are part of every trip.

Don't avoid the failure. Use it as a springboard to your success.

As you go through your day today, don't stop, and fail your way to the top.

Today's the day!

YOUR GOLDMINE

YOU MAY HAVE NEVER HEARD OF ROBERT ARMSTRONG, BUT you've probably heard of an idea he captured and maximized. Robert Armstrong was a struggling cartoonist and graphic artist. During a low point in his career, he spent most of his days sitting on the sofa watching daytime TV. A good friend called him one day, and in an attempt to be humorous said, "How's my favorite couch potato?"

Neither of the friends had ever heard that term before, and after their conversation, Robert Armstrong hung up the phone and thought about the idea of a couch potato. He started drawing cartoons, capturing his idea, and then he trademarked the term couch potato. Ironically, out of the lowest point in his career, came his goldmine. It only had value to him because he recognized it. Otherwise, you and I would have never heard of a couch potato.

In his classic book *Acres of Diamonds*, Russell Conwell described a frustrated African farmer who sold his family farm to seek his fortune hunting for diamonds in South Africa. Several years later, broke and dejected, he returned to the farm he had once owned simply hoping to get a job as a laborer only to find that the very farm he had once owned had become the site of one of the most prosperous diamond mines in the world.

The farmer had never realized that some of those annoying rocks he had removed from his fields while plowing were actually raw diamonds. He had left his life as a farmer to search for diamonds without even knowing what diamonds looked like.

You and I are sitting on our own goldmines whether we recognize them or not. We must understand that great ideas rarely come packaged as great ideas. They are most often disguised as problems or challenges. The whole world is looking for a great idea and trips over one several times each week without even recognizing it.

The only thing you need to do to have a great idea is to simply go through your daily routine, wait for something bad to happen, and consider how you could have avoided that. The answer is a great idea. To take the process one step further, all you need to do to have a great business is to consider how you can help other people avoid that problem.

The world will give you fame, fortune, and everything you seek if you will help them solve their problems; but if you won't recognize couch potatoes, raw diamonds, or the proverbial goldmines in your own life, you will be frustrated in your search to find the things you already have.

As you go through your day today, seek the opportunities that are within your reach right now.

Today's the day!

Transformation

Transformation is more about the questions you are willing to ask yourself than the answers you think you already know.

We live in a material world in which people seek instant gratification. They want to measure themselves based on what they have instead of who they are or what they do. What we have is a poor indicator of ourselves. The best indicator of success is simply who we are. This indicator is made up of the elements of our character, our personality, and our principles. The measure of who we are will lead to the second indicator, which is what we do. In this arena, we are judged by our efficiency, our productivity, and the contribution we make to the world. Only after we determine who we are and what we do can we impact what we have; but in our instant gratification world, people who are not willing to change any elements of their personality or their performance simply want to have the rewards.

This is why there are many more lottery tickets sold than personal development books. Ironically, even when people defy the odds and win the lottery, if they haven't altered who they are or what they do, they will inevitably lose what they have.

If you have land that grows trees that produces fruit, the long-term value cannot be determined solely by the fruit or even the trees. The land is the core value. If you are a person of principle and character who performs efficiently and productively, you will have the rewards that everyone seeks; and even if you lost your rewards, you would still be able to reproduce the results just as if one year's crop of fruit is ruined, there will be a crop the following year. Or even if the trees are destroyed, they can be replaced or regrown as long as the core value of the land is retained.

If people who want to be instant millionaires would transform their thinking to first become a millionaire personality with a millionaire mindset, then they would perform tasks that generate millions of dollars of value into the marketplace. This would result in them being millionaires many times over. But if you just want the fruit without the land or the trees, any success you enjoy will be short-lived.

Success comes from being, then doing, which results in having. If you simply want to have more things without transforming who you are as a person and what you do as a service to the world, you are doomed to failure.

As you go through your day today, remember to focus on who you are and what you do and then you will have everything you desire.

Today's the day!

LONG LIVE THE KING

ONE DAY IN MAY 2015, LIKE MILLIONS OF PEOPLE AROUND THE world, I woke up to the sad news that B.B. King had died. Any time you have an aging hero, you know that fateful day is inevitable, but you're never quite ready. I have long been an admirer of anyone who is the best at whatever they have chosen to do in their life. For 70 years, B.B. King was, quite simply, the best.

As a teenager in the 1970s, I came to admire a number of my generation's great guitarists, including Eric Clapton, Jimi Hendrix, Jimmy Page, Carlos Santana, and many others. When I studied their biographies or news stories about them, they inevitably all named B.B. King as their greatest influence. I heard him play in concert a number of times and was ecstatic when he agreed to include his biggest hit, *The Thrill is Gone*, in the movie *The Ultimate Gift* based on my novel.

Recently in the field of personal achievement, the theory has emerged that if you perform a task for 10,000 hours you become an expert and will be judged to be among the best in the world. If this is true, B.B. King came by his fame and fortune honestly. Many people claim the title, but B.B. King was "the hardest working man in show business." In 1956, B.B.

King and his band played 342 one-nighters. When asked about his torturous schedule, the blues legend was heard to say, "It beats picking cotton," which is something he knew a lot about.

B.B. King was born in the Mississippi Delta in 1925. He began picking cotton at age seven as he and his family were sharecroppers. He continued to tour well past his 80th birthday and even in 2014 was reported to play over 100 dates. He was long past needing any more fortune or fame. It was simply a matter of the fact that B.B. King loved to play his famous guitar "Lucille" and make crowds around the world happy.

He was inducted into the Blues and Rock and Roll Hall of Fame and received the Presidential Medal of Freedom from President George W. Bush. He presented one of his guitars to Pope John Paul II and sang a duet with President Barack Obama.

Anyone who wants to be the best at anything has to have that kind of joy and passion for that which they pursue. In this way, B.B. King leaves a legacy of his music and is an example to us all.

As you go through your day today, pursue your passion, and take a moment to listen to B.B. King.

Today's the day!

THE POWER OF PESSIMISM

FOR SEVERAL DECADES, THROUGH MY WEEKLY COLUMNS AS well as my books, movies, and speeches, I have endeavored to convince people that having a positive attitude, focusing their energy, and acting upon their motivations can bring positive results in their lives and the people around them.

My late, great colleague, mentor, and friend Zig Ziglar was fond of saying, "I'm an optimist. I would go after Moby Dick in a rowboat and take the tartar sauce with me."

Unfortunately, our society seems to be predominantly populated by people who do not believe that being an optimist is worthwhile. Many of these individuals communicate to me that motivation and a positive attitude are just smoke and mirrors that might create temporary euphoria or warm, fuzzy feelings but don't really matter in the real world.

Sometimes it's easier to prove the opposite side of an argument. According to recent research conducted by Dr. Michael Scheier, "In general, pessimists don't perform as well in life as optimists. They tend to deny, avoid, and distort the problems they confront and dwell on their negative feelings." Dr.

Scheier cites five specific scientifically provable results of being a pessimist.

1. Pessimism kills your creativity. We always find what we're looking for, and pessimists seem to focus on negative results or nothing at all which does not promote innovative creative thinking. The research also shows that pessimists hinder the creativity of colleagues, friends, and family members around them.

2. Pessimism harms you emotionally. The scientific study indicates that while motivation wears off and has to be renewed constantly, pessimism actually sticks with you and is reinforced when you have a fleeting negative thought. This brief shot of pessimism can instantly bring back all of the negative thoughts and emotions you have had and can stay with you long term.

3. Pessimism hurts you professionally. The statistics show that your attitude will affect your measureable performance on the job and will impact those around you negatively. This poor performance and bad attitude will keep you from promotions and bonuses while moving you ever closer to the unemployment line.

4. Pessimism damages relationships. Your friends and loved ones may not even directly notice your pessimism, but they will be aware of how they feel when they are around you or immediately after they have

been in your presence. We subconsciously judge others by how they make us feel.

5. Pessimism makes you sick. You've heard of the placebo effect which causes people to get better because they think they're going to get better whether the treatment they are receiving is valid or not. The scientists studying pessimism came up with a term they call "nocebo" which, basically, indicates that if you think you're going to feel bad you will, and if you believe you're going to get sick, you will likely be proven correct. The research went on to show that pessimism can lead directly to heart attacks and other serious problems including dementia.

If I haven't convinced you to be an optimist yet, I hope the current scientific research will at least motivate you to stop being a pessimist.

As you go through your day today, avoid the power of pessimism—be optimistic and live well.

Today's the day!

SIMPLIFY AND SUCCEED

I HAVE WORKED IN AND AROUND THE FINANCIAL AND INVEST-ment industry for my entire career. I began by running my own office with a New York Stock Exchange member firm, then went into financial planning, and now, through my books, movies, speeches, and these columns, I advise people around the world on the attitudes that will make their money work as hard for them as they worked for their money.

I'm a firm believer that even if you work with a money manager, broker, estate planner, or other financial professional, you need to manage your own money. The most common reaction I receive to that statement is, "I don't understand it, so I let someone else handle it." I don't disagree with letting someone else handle it, and I even find it advisable to have professionals on your team, but I reject the notion that people who are smart enough to earn money aren't smart enough to manage it or invest it.

Too many people in the financial service industry and other professions believe their career is more valid if they somehow make their profession more mysterious and confusing. In this way, these misguided individuals feel that you will trust them to handle it because they understand it and you don't. This is counterproductive and a recipe for disaster.

Confusion creates doubt, and doubt creates procrastination. Procrastination is the enemy of any investment or financial plan. Time is your ally, and if you don't use all of it to your benefit, you won't be as successful as you otherwise could be.

If your doctor, lawyer, car mechanic, or financial professional can't explain things to you so that you can be a part of the decision-making process, there's nothing wrong with you, it's just that they are not a true professional. A great physician should be able to explain your diagnosis and treatment in terms that you understand. You shouldn't have to go to medical school or law school to communicate with the professionals you hire to assist you in succeeding.

Warren Buffett, whom I consider among the world's greatest investors, relies upon a series of criteria he has developed as an investor for over half-a-century. Among Mr. Buffett's criteria is "Don't invest in things you don't understand." One of the greatest upward moves in the world's equity markets has come to be known as "the dot com boom of the 1990s." Many investors' portfolios benefitted greatly from the rapid growth of hardware and software corporations around the world. Warren Buffett predominantly ignored these high-tech opportunities because he simply didn't feel he understood them. Buffett continued to successfully invest in railroads, airlines, energy companies, and other opportunities he understood and that made him a multi-billionaire.

If you are a professional in any area of endeavor, it's your job to make complex concepts simple to those you serve, and you need to make sure that those who serve you do the same.

As you go through your day today, eliminate complexity and succeed through simplicity.

Today's the day!

FINITE RESOURCES

Two out of Three

ONE OF THE MOST QUESTIONABLE ADVERTISING, MARKETING, or promotional phrases is, "You can have it all." You can have all of some things and more of other things, but you can't have all of everything.

Time, energy, and money are all finite resources. Wealth brings you choices, but the ability to choose "all of the above" doesn't exist. I believe if you're producing any product or service, your results can be fast, good, or cheap. You can pick two out of three, but you can't have them all. If you want something fast and good, it will be expensive. If you want something fast and cheap, it will not be good.

When you're investing your money, you can invest for safety, liquidity, or return. There's no right answer, and any of these goals will be appropriate for certain investors at various times of their lives; however, once again, you can't have it all. If you want total safety, you will have to give up some liquidity and some return. If, on the other hand, you want the highest possible return, you will forego liquidity and safety; important decisions in your personal life, therefore, are not yes or no. They are top five or top ten type of decisions.

We often overlook issues of health, family, spirituality, and well-being when we establish our priorities. All things being equal, more money is better than less money, but if you're sacrificing your health or quality time with your loved ones for money, it is likely a poor bargain; we must, therefore, budget the things that are finite such as our time and money while prioritizing the elements of life that are infinite such as spirituality, well-being, and significance.

A veteran airline pilot once told me that on a four-hour, coast-to-coast flight, we would be off-course at least three-and-one-half hours of the entire trip. Our lives are much the same way in that success involves a constant adjustment and precise management of all elements. We live in a high-definition movie environment, not a single-frame snapshot photo. The right priorities and percentages for me would likely be improper for you, and even if you have perfect balance today, it probably won't fit for you next week, next month, or next year.

Wisdom comes not only from making good decisions but in deciding how to decide.

As you go through your day today, realize you can't have it all, so get what matters most to you.

Today's the day!

STEERING WHEEL UNIVERSITY

I HEARD TWO SEPARATE NEWS STORIES WITHIN TEN MINUTES of one another. Individually, these two stories were interesting, but combined, they can be impactful.

The first story described the recent study from the U.S. Department of Transportation that indicates that the average working person spends over an hour a day commuting or otherwise driving their car for errands, work-related responsibilities, and other random trips. The second news story highlighted research that revealed that anyone who reads one hour per day on any topic will become an expert on that subject within three years.

People who have knowledge internalize facts, while people who have wisdom combine facts and use them in the real world.

As a blind person myself who has authored more than 30 books and am approaching writing a thousand weekly columns, as mentioned previously, when I could read with my eyes, I doubt I ever read a whole book cover-to-cover. Now, as a blind person for over a quarter of a century, I average reading one book a day. This is accomplished utilizing high-speed audio books, which I believe to be a vastly superior way to assimilate knowledge once you get accustomed to it.

Reading approximately 8,000 books over the past 25 years has changed my life. Becoming a reader made me want to be a writer, and exposing myself to the greatest minds the world has ever known has opened my life, both personally and professionally, to a world of possibilities.

If you will consider the time you spend driving your car, exercising, doing work around the house or yard, along with any other physical tasks that do not require your listening attention, you will find that you have the capacity to read more than 99 percent of people in the world. This enhanced level of learning cannot only change your life but the lives of those around you as you grow and develop.

Time and money are our two main finite resources that impact us the most. Any time we can find free time or money, we have to consider putting it to work for us. If you have access to a 401K or other retirement accounts with matching funds, this is free money that you should put to work for your future. If you spend regular time each week engaged in physical activities that would allow you to listen to audio books or teaching courses, you should recapture these lost minutes and hours. They can change your world.

As you go through your day today, consider the idle time you have, and get engaged.

Today's the day!

CRAZY AND WISE

FOR THE PAST 27 YEARS, I HAVE RUN THE NARRATIVE TELEVIsion Network that makes movies, television, and other educational programming accessible to 13 million blind and visually impaired Americans and many millions more around the world. I founded NTN out of my own need, not any knowledge or expertise I had at that time because I, quite simply, didn't have any. Today, I look back on our company's growth and success in awe and wonder. We have received an Emmy Award, an International Film and Video Award, and the Media Access Award from the broadcast and cable industry. As I look back on our accomplishments, I am struck by how little we knew when we began.

Steve Jobs may have said it best when he declared, "The ones who are crazy enough to think that they can change the world are the ones who do."

Knowing what you want to do and why you want to do it are infinitely more valuable than understanding how to do something. My late, great friend, colleague, and mentor Dr. Robert Schuller was fond of saying, "Never let how you are going to do it get mixed up in what you are going to do."

The people we call experts are those who have the best understanding of the current state-of-the-art. These experts' livelihood, fame, and acclaim come from knowing how things are today and what makes them work; these individuals are, therefore, consciously or unconsciously reluctant to stretch the bounds of possibility as it might relate to breakthrough ideas presented by others. All innovation, invention, and development does not fit into the current world; therefore, if you ask one of these experts about doing something that's never been done, it is highly likely that you are going to get a negative response.

As I look back on my career in the broadcast, cable, and streaming industries during a time of rapid transition and innovation, I remain grateful that I was clueless. People who can best describe why things work today are often not the best people to evaluate how things might work in the future. When you do find it necessary to seek advice or counsel from people who are experts, it is far better to ask them how they would implement your idea and make it work rather than to ask them if they believe your idea will work.

The late, great entrepreneur and executive Mary Kay Ash said, "People will support that which they help to create." We must use the expertise of others sparingly and wisely. Someone who knows it all today will be a washed-up antique in a few short years. Those who will succeed in the future will focus more on possibility than on reality.

As you go through your day today, be crazy like Steve Jobs and others who have changed the world.

Today's the day!

DON'T BE AN IDIOT

I AM PRIVILEGED TO BE A PROFESSIONAL SPEAKER. IT HAS GIVEN me the ability to share my message with millions of people in arena events and business conventions around the world. Among the many great things about being a professional speaker are the wonderful colleagues I get to work with. I have shared the stage with Zig Ziglar, Christopher Reeve, Colin Powell, Dr. Denis Waitley, Tony Robbins, Paul Harvey, Dr. Robert Schuller, and many others.

One of my most unique colleagues is a talented speaker named Larry Winget. Most professional speakers take the stage wearing their best suit or professional attire. I have never known Larry to wear a tie if he even owns one. Many years ago, he shaved his head and began appearing onstage with flamboyant glasses, earrings, and often with a toilet plunger affixed to his bald head.

Over the years, people have labeled me as a motivational speaker. Larry Winget proudly proclaims himself to be an irritational speaker. While I encourage my audiences with phrases such as, "You are one quality decision away from anything you want," and "You change your life when you change your mind," Larry regularly confronts his audiences with one of his trademark statements, "If you're not where you want to be, it's because you're lazy, stupid, or don't give a blank."

Larry and I collaborated, along with the talented author Sharon Lechter on an audio series from Napoleon Hill entitled *17 Principles of Success*. In this project, Larry and I went back and forth recording our thoughts on the relevance of Napoleon Hill's financial principles in the 21st century. After we finished the project, I was struck by the fact that Larry and I are complete opposites but worked very well together. While I was thinking about this, Larry actually called me and suggested the two of us team up on another audio program. The recording that came from that idea is now known as *Motivation and Irritation*.

As Larry and I were chatting back and forth preparing to do the recording, he mentioned his son had just left home for college, and he'd had the opportunity to spend quite a bit of time with his son during the last few days he was living at home. I asked Larry, as a great author and speaker, if he had any advice for his son as the young man was leaving home to complete his education and move out into the world. Larry responded automatically sharing the advice he gave his son. "Don't be an idiot." While my immediate thought was how inappropriate Larry's statement to his son might have been, upon further reflection, I realized that it's powerful advice for that young man as well as you and me.

We live in a world where your best efforts, your reputation, and your life's work can be wiped out with one brief lapse of judgment. If you will remember that all guns are loaded, all microphones are turned on, and you're responsible for everything you do even if you're drunk, you will avoid many pitfalls.

Our parents and grandparents could often get away with briefly being an idiot, but here in the 21st century, everyone everywhere is armed with a cell phone that functions as a video camera. If you do let down your guard and act as if you're an idiot, it will not go unnoticed or be forgotten. It will likely be a permanent fixture on the World Wide Web.

As you go through your day today, work hard, treat people well, and don't be an idiot.

Today's the day!

FREEDOM AND SUCCESS

FOR ALMOST 20 YEARS, MY COLUMN HAS BEEN READ EACH WEEK by people around the world. The readers of the *Winners' Wisdom* columns represent a multitude of nationalities, faiths, creeds, and cultures.

If you have been a reader of mine for any length of time, you know that I believe that our success is greatly a product of our own attitude, effort, and ingenuity; however, this belief presumes that you live in a free and open society.

In the two decades I have been writing *Winners' Wisdom,* technology has changed the world. In the mid-1990s, most of the readers of my weekly columns accessed my message via a print publication such as a magazine or newspaper. Today because of the Internet, a diverse group of people around the globe read this weekly offering via the Internet. Many of these new online readers live in countries where they face resistance and oppression toward their success, freedom, and happiness.

Freedom is an often-misunderstood word. We all grasp the concept of being able to do what we want to do and when we want to do it, but our ideas of freedom often get confused when we think of other people's liberty, particularly when it relates to those with whom we disagree. The great American patriot, Thomas Paine, said, "He who would make his own liberty secure must guard even his own enemy from oppression."

If you and I believe in liberty and enjoy our own freedom to succeed or fail on our own terms, we must not only tolerate those with whom we disagree, but we must be willing to fight for their rights as well as our own. I believe a true patriot and lover of liberty should be able to readily identify and articulate several beliefs, positions, and practices they disagree with personally but would defend vigorously.

I'm a voracious reader and find that I gain more enlightenment and deeper learning when reading books written by authors with whom I disagree. In many cases, I find that our areas of disagreement aren't as deep as I thought they were, and as I begin to understand the motives behind other people's mission and message, I find a lot of common ground. There is a phrase generally attributed to Native American wisdom that says, "Don't judge a man unless you have walked a mile in his moccasins."

Many times issues boil down to right versus wrong; in which case, we must stand up for what is right. But sometimes that which we think is wrong is merely a different perspective.

As you go through your day today, celebrate your own freedom by protecting the freedom of others.

Today's the day!

An Unlikely War Hero

I READ ABOUT THE EXPLOITS OF A MAN WHO SERVED DURING World War II who may well have had more to do with the allied victory than any other single person. Abraham Wald used his talents, abilities, and gifts to save countless lives and turn the tide of the war. He did not serve in the European Theater nor in the Pacific. He never confronted the Nazis or the Japanese. He never held a gun, dropped a bomb, or drove a tank. Abraham Wald never even went through basic training and served out the war in an apartment in New York City.

Abraham Wald was arguably the most gifted mathematician of his generation. He was not only adept at coming up with the right answers to complex problems, Abraham Wald had a skill for identifying the right questions.

The allied air command faced a logistical dilemma throughout the war. Air superiority was the key to victory in both the conflict against Germany as well as Japan. Each pilot and plane was worth their weight in gold to the war effort. The difficult decision was where and how much armor should be put on each plane. The armor they used was very thick and heavy sheets of metal that were placed at strategic locations on each aircraft. If there was too much armor, the planes could not take off or would waste precious fuel. If there was not enough armor, the planes were shot down.

The generals made diagrams of the bullet holes in each plane as they returned from their missions. They found that the bullet holes were concentrated along the wings and fuselage of the planes with very little damage done to the cockpit area or the engine compartment. Previous to the study, all of the armor had been positioned around the cockpit and engine to protect the pilot and the motor that flew the plane.

The generals enlisted the help of Abraham Wald to determine how the armor could be moved to protect the fuselage and wings since the other more vital areas were rarely being hit anyway. It was at that point that the wisdom and genius of Abraham Wald won the war. Wald accurately informed the aviation experts that they needed to keep protecting the areas of the returning planes that weren't being hit because they weren't studying the planes that would tell the whole story. Abraham Wald went on to explain that the planes that were shot down had been hit in the cockpit or engine, and they never returned to be studied.

In-depth research after the war estimated that without Wald's wisdom and intervention, the armor in our aircraft would have been moved to the wings and fuselage, and our superior air power would have been decimated within a few short months—quite possibly changing the outcome of the war. Wald understood that the right answer to the wrong question can be misleading and sometimes deadly.

As you go through your day today, seek the right answers to the right questions.

Today's the day!

Fundamental Attribution

WE ALL NATURALLY SEE THE ENTIRE WORLD FROM OUR OWN unique perspective. We view the actions of others as they relate to us. There is a phrase that has slipped into the vernacular of our culture recently that is powerful to keep in mind: "It's not about you."

Psychologists often refer to the principle of fundamental attribution. Simply stated, we assume that everything around us is caused by us, meant for us, and aimed at us. This is, most often, not the case. When people you confront are rude to you, cut you off in traffic, or ignore you entirely as you pass by them, it rarely, if ever, has anything to do with you.

We produced a movie entitled *The Ultimate Legacy* based on my novel *The Gift of a Legacy*. This is the third movie in *The Ultimate Gift* trilogy, and we added Raquel Welch to the list of cast members who had already been in the first two films. Raquel Welch plays a complex character who has just learned she has a terminal disease and may only have a short time to live.

The Ultimate Legacy was shot in a small town in Kentucky. Our cast, crew, and the residents of that small town were all excited to get to see and meet Raquel Welch. Several people initially thought Miss Welch was rude or standoffish until they later understood her attitude had nothing to do with them but was simply a matter of her preparing to do her lines, playing a scene in which she was just informed she was dying.

People with disabilities or those who are members of a minority group too often attribute rude behavior or bad service to their race, color, or disability, when in reality, rude behavior and bad service have become commonplace and touch us all every day. Our natural reaction to being confronted by these unfortunate behaviors is to treat others the way we are being treated instead of the way we would like to be treated. How we treat others is as much a reflection of how we feel about ourselves as how we feel about those around us.

Before you diminish yourself and hurt others around you, it's at least worth asking a benign question. If you're being treated poorly, stop, take a deep breath, and inquire whether you've done something to elicit the other person's behavior. You will be shocked to learn that the poor behavior you thought was directed at you was caused by a myriad of factors, and "It's not about you."

As you go through your day today, assume the best—at least until you can confirm the worst.

Today's the day!

SMELL THE COFFEE

IN OUR FREE MARKET SOCIETY, WE SUCCEED BY CREATING value in the lives of other people. Whatever product or service you are part of delivering, you must give people more value in their minds than the price they are paying you. I find that in my own business, I enjoy delivering a high-level product or service that is sold on value and not price. This can be accomplished in almost any field.

Coffee beans are a commodity. They are traded electronically on the world markets, and the price fluctuates constantly by fractions of a penny. If you are offering coffee beans as a commodity, it can be difficult to differentiate your organization from your competitor's. If you offer coffee by the cup at a convenience store or a drive-through, you are offering a service. People who could brew their own coffee for a few cents are willing to pay you a few dollars for the convenience and service you provide. As long as your coffee is hot and fresh, it will meet the needs of your customers. Beyond that, it is hard to stand out from the crowd.

Beyond providing a commodity or a service, there's one additional element you can provide that can make you totally unique and world-renowned. You can offer the same cup of coffee but make it an experience. People who would only pay a few pennies for coffee beans on the open market, or a few dollars for a cup of coffee to go at the gas station, will pay hundreds of times the price of coffee beans to drink the same beverage if it is part of an experience. Whether you're sitting at a sidewalk café in Paris, listening to jazz musicians in New Orleans, or watching the ships come in under the Golden Gate Bridge, a cup of coffee can be infinitely more than ground beans and hot water. People rarely applaud or sing the praises of a commodity or even a service, but they will spread the news about an experience for years.

A limousine experience is little more than a taxi with a great driver who's informed, engaged, and professional. A bartender can be so much more than someone who simply pours beverages when he or she remembers your name, your preferences, and provides compelling conversation. An insurance or financial broker who remembers as much about your kids and your hobbies as they do about their own products goes from being a sales person to a valued part of your family.

As you go through your day today, use commodities that provide a service in order to create an experience.

Today's the day!

Applied Absurdity

THERE ARE TIMES WE NEED STRUCTURE, TIMES TO THINK OUT-
side the box, and then, every once in a while, you simply need
to apply some absurdity.

Our business within the television industry was undergoing
some pricing pressure. We were on the bad side of the supply/
demand curve, and it created a dilemma for the bottom line.
At one point, I heard myself say, "We need to get paid more for
doing less and serve our clients better." I actually laughed aloud
at the absurdity of the statement, but then I asked the ques-
tion that is the beginning of all innovation. "What if this were
possible?" The end result was that we developed a multilayered
service for which we get paid more money while providing an
enhanced product to our audience.

I met a gentleman who had lost his job and was within a
few weeks of being kicked out of his apartment. He said, some-
what sarcastically, "I need someone to pay me to live in their
apartment." He laughed aloud, but I didn't join in and simply
asked, "Where are some places where that might be possible?"
The bottom line is that within a few weeks, he had found a job

managing a ministorage facility where they pay him a salary and provide him with a very nice apartment to live onsite.

A big dream doesn't cost any more than a little one. If you think like everyone else, you will find yourself waiting at the end of a very long line that ends at the door of mediocrity. If you will think out of the box or even absurdly, you will often find yourself standing alone atop the mountain everyone else is trying to climb.

If you ever come to our office at the Narrative Television Network, you will see scores of autographed photos of movie stars in the lobby. These are actresses and actors who have given me interviews or appeared in our programming. Many industry people wonder how we got so many of the A-list celebrities to be part of our work. The very simple answer is, "I asked them."

The ancient wisdom tells us that you have not because you ask not. Sometimes when we ask for something, the answer is no, but if we don't ask, the answer is always no.

As you go through your day today, leave *ordinary* behind and think *absurdly*.

Today's the day!

THE MOST VALUABLE COMMODITIES

IDEAS, INNOVATIONS, AND INVENTIONS

THE MOST VALUABLE COMMODITY IN THE WORLD MAY WELL BE an idea. A revolutionary new concept can change your life, change your business, and sometimes change the world.

New ideas involve both the art and the science of creativity. We must think in new and different ways, but sometimes ideas are elusive, and we must wait for the intersection of the right time and the right place. While ideas may take a unique set of circumstances, innovation can be available for us to consider and explore at any time.

For several centuries, the item we call a suitcase existed pretty much in the same basic form and style we know it today. Then, a half-a-century ago, someone came up with the innovation of putting wheels on a suitcase. They did not have the idea to invent a suitcase. They simply had an innovation to make the existing suitcase better. The original innovation involved putting wheels on the bottom of a suitcase so it stood up much as it had done for centuries, but now it had wheels on the bottom. The challenge was that this suitcase could be pulled by a handle or a strap but consistently tipped over because it was top heavy. It took several decades before someone came up with the innovation of putting wheels on the edge and installing an extending handle. This innovation is what we now call a roller board. It has revolutionized the luggage industry.

The reason the original innovation involved putting the wheels on the bottom was simply because that's the way a standard suitcase was visualized by everyone. It took someone who could mentally turn the suitcase on its edge and, thereby, change the industry.

While you're waiting for your big idea, consider innovating the existing world around you. What can you transform, transfer, translate, or make transparent? Think of new uses for products that already exist.

My core business involves making movies and television accessible for millions of blind and visually impaired people by inserting narration between existing dialogue to describe the visual elements of the program. For years, people asked me if this could be done for live theatre. It didn't seem possible immediately because there was no videotape or digital program file on which to record the narration voice.

Then there came the day I was in Mexico giving a speech for a number of business leaders. About half my audience was Spanish speaking, and as I was giving my speech, a gentleman at the edge of the stage was quietly translating my words into Spanish and speaking into a microphone. The microphone was connected to a low-power FM transmitter, and throughout the amphitheater, Spanish-speaking people had small transistor radios the size of a deck of cards in their pockets and were listening to my speech being translated into Spanish via a small earpiece.

As I was standing there speaking about the concept of being open to opportunities, it dawned on me that a device for translating foreign languages was also a device for narrating for blind and visually impaired theatre audiences. My entire innovation involved using existing technology for a different use. The only thing that changed was my own perspective.

Perspective is a good tool to orient us as to where we are, but it is often a barrier keeping us from where we could be.

As you go through your day today, change your perspective, and change the world.

Today's the day!

RESILIENCE

I BELIEVE ONE OF THE MOST IMPORTANT CHARACTERISTICS that any person can have is that of resilience. Resilience is that quality that allows us to be knocked down and get up again, and again, and again. Being knocked down is not an interruption in our life but is simply part of life. Often the act of getting up and going on makes us stronger and allows us to climb farther and faster toward success. The next time you get knocked down personally or professionally, remember to react, reflect, and recommit.

Some people would tell you to avoid negative thoughts or bitter reactions to a setback. This is not natural, normal, or even possible. We will always react to adversity. I think it is imperative that we both control and limit this reaction. Give yourself permission for an hour or even a day to react with anger, grief, or bitterness; but then put an end to it and go to the next phase which is reflection.

When we reflect on our setbacks or adversity, we can consider what we did to cause the situation, what we can do in the future to avoid the situation, and what other people have done to overcome and triumph after similar setbacks. This reflecting phase gets us out of the immediate reaction and allows us to take control and create a learning experience that will be an asset for our success in the future.

After we have controlled our reaction and learned from reflection, we must recommit to our goals and objectives. This process of recommitting is what separates winners from losers. The winners in life get back on the path to their original goal or sometimes even a loftier goal. Often as we reflect on the setback and see how others have handled a similar situation, we realize that there is more potential than we had originally thought, and the possibilities are greater than we had considered.

When we can react, reflect, and recommit, we begin to see setbacks as opportunities. Often when we succeed, we look back from the perspective of the mountaintop and realize that the setbacks we suffered were the fertilizer for greater growth and bigger success.

As you go through your day today, never retreat. Simply react, reflect, and recommit.

Today's the day!

PULLING THE TRIGGER

WE SUCCEED BASED ON WHAT WE DO—NOT WHAT WE THOUGHT about doing, meant to do, wanted to do, or intended to do. Great ideas, thoughts, and goals are worthless without action. It all comes down to that vital element of pulling the trigger. The critical component of pulling the trigger is timing. We have all known of people who get the reputation of going off "halfcocked." These people act upon a whim and rarely consider the cost or the consequences.

We must evaluate every decision before we act. It's not only whether our actions will result in something good, but there's the question of whether we could be doing something better with the same time, effort, and energy. In this way, good can often become the enemy of great. While it is foolish to act before we have engaged in our thought process, it is wasteful not to act once we have.

Adlai Stevenson was an articulate politician and diplomat. He believed in acting upon his principles and said, "On the plains of hesitation lie the blackened bones of countless millions who, at the dawn of victory, lay down to rest, and in resting died."

If you look outside of yourself at the prevailing conditions, business climate, and other factors, it may never seem like the right time to take action; but if you will look inside of yourself, your own motivation, inspiration, and powerful emotion can make it the perfect time to pull the trigger.

Thoughts, ideas, and inspiration are gifts we have received. We must protect, preserve, and utilize these gifts carefully. Whenever you have a thought about doing something, whether it's as lofty as starting a new business, writing a book, or taking your life in a new direction, or whether it's as simple as calling an old friend, connecting with a new mentor, or committing to read a particular book, you must take action.

Every idea you have and every thought you can capture should go through your evaluation process to determine how to proceed. My thoughts and ideas all fall into one of several categories. Either they are put on my "to-do list" for that day; they are entered into my calendar to be done at some point in the future; they are put in a pending file to be reconsidered at another time; or they are flushed out of my mind to be replaced by more productive and valuable ideas and pursuits.

Procrastination is the main ingredient in the recipe for failure, but if you take a great idea you have today, judge its value, consider it among your priorities, and determine to reevaluate it next week, you're not procrastinating; but if you don't capture that idea or thought somewhere, it will drift off into the void from whence it came.

As you go through your day today, capture great ideas, evaluate them, and pull the trigger.

Today's the day!

Money Can Make You Happy

I'VE HEARD IT SAID COUNTLESS WAYS THROUGHOUT MY LIFE that "Money won't make you happy." While I agree that the mere act of possessing money won't, in and of itself, make you happy, utilizing money properly can.

When we think back on our lives about when we were truly happy, we discover it was at the times when we were expending our effort and energy in serving others and making them happy. Happiness is an elusive concept. To the extent we try to create it for ourselves, it avoids us, but to the extent we try to create happiness for others, it engulfs us. If we are committed to spending our time and effort to serving others and making them happy, and if we then add money to that equation, we can make many more people, and in turn ourselves, very happy.

There are only three things we can do with our money: invest it, spend it, or give it away. A portion of every dollar should be directed toward each of these areas. Money that we spend today can meet our current needs and the needs of those around us. Money that we invest can meet these same needs in the future. But money we give away can make us happy now, for the rest of our lives, and leave a legacy behind long after we are gone.

Giving money away productively and effectively is not as easy as it would seem. Bill Gates said, "Giving money away properly is more difficult than earning the money in the first place." Since no one alive today knows more about earning money than Bill Gates, we should all value his judgment on giving.

The best gift you can give yourself and your loved ones utilizing money is an emergency fund. The majority of stress, abuse, and divorce in our society is created by money problems. Most of these problems could be avoided with an emergency fund consisting of six months' worth of your average living expenses. Beyond this and meeting your basic needs, the money we give away should continue to give.

If you forego a luxury item you want and give to someone else so that they can buy a luxury item for themselves that doesn't impact anyone else, you will not make yourself or the person receiving your gift as happy as could have otherwise been possible; however, if you give gifts to people who utilize that gift to serve others in a way that can impact society into the future, you can multiply and share the happiness money generates. Whether it's time, love, resources, or money, the way to enjoy it best is to share it with others.

As you go through your day today, be happy as you use your money, time, and talent to make others happy.

Today's the day!

PROBLEMS AND POSSIBILITIES

THIS COLUMN IS READ EACH WEEK BY COUNTLESS PEOPLE IN newspapers, magazines, and online publications around the world. I have been writing these weekly columns for almost 20 years, and therefore, have written approximately 1,000 installments of *Winners' Wisdom*. These columns have filled three books to date with more planned for the future.

I do a 30-minute national radio show as well as a local program in my hometown based on each week's column. The question I'm most often asked about *Winners' Wisdom* is, "Where do you get the ideas for all of your columns?" A lady in Australia who reads *Winners' Wisdom* each week forwarded a quote to me from author Simon Sinek who may have said it best: "If everything goes right, we get a good experience. If everything goes wrong, we get a good story!"

I see problems, challenges, and difficulties as a never-ending resource for subject matter within these weekly columns. To change your problems into resources, opportunities, and possibilities, you need to change your internal dialogue. The next time you're confronted with a problem, avoid the question that pops into all of our minds at that moment, which is the age-old lament, *Why me?* When you choose to view the problem as an opportunity, your first question will be, *Why not me?* followed by the quality questions, *Why did this happen? How can this be overcome? How can this be avoided?* and finally, *How can I help other people avoid or overcome this problem?* The answers to these quality questions can create powerful ideas, concepts, and even business opportunities.

In our society, we succeed by solving problems for others. The bigger the problems we solve and the more people for whom we solve problems, the more we are compensated. Sanitation workers solve the problems that are created when garbage is left lying around too long. They are compensated for solving this problem. Heart surgeons solve life-and-death problems and are more highly compensated; however, I know people who own refuse companies and remove the garbage of millions of people, and they earn many times more money than a heart surgeon. The key is to always be a problem solver.

Looking at problems as resources and potential opportunities, you will begin to change your dialogue with others and find yourself asking questions like, *Do you have any challenges I can assist with?* or *What's your biggest problem, and how can I help?* or *What are the long-term obstacles that keep you up at night?* The world will give you fame, fortune, and acclaim if you will just help them solve their problems.

As you go through your day today, remember that the solution you are seeking is hiding in plain sight disguised as a problem.

Today's the day!

Movers and Shakers

You've probably heard it said, "It's not what you know. It's who you know." I'm a firm believer that both are important.

My company, Narrative Television Network, makes movies, television, and educational programming accessible for the 13 million blind and visually-impaired Americans and their families as well as millions more around the world. When I first began the company over 25 years ago, I hosted a brief talk show before and after each program to introduce the show, interview some of the stars, and fill some of the network time so all of our stations across the country would be synched. These talk shows were taped in a studio in Washington, DC. That same studio produced another program called *Washington Reporter*, and the CEO of the studio asked me if I would be willing to cohost *Washington Reporter* as well as the Narrative TV update. I agreed, and for two years enjoyed interviewing people including Senator Ted Kennedy, Dr. Henry Kissinger, and many others.

We were having some challenges with the Federal Communications Commission in getting our Narrative Television delivered to stations across the country, and I was thinking about it one day as I interviewed Ron Nessen who had been the press secretary at the White House during President Ford's administration. After the interview, Mr. Nessen and I were in the makeup room at the same time having our makeup removed, and I shared my frustration with him. He agreed to have breakfast with me the next morning to discuss my challenges.

Over breakfast, I shared with him my goals of making narrated programming and the Narrative Television Network as readily available in every part of the country as closed captioning was for deaf individuals. After explaining to Mr. Nessen the complexity of my problems, I was shocked when he summed it up by saying, "Your problem is very simple. Nobody cares." I argued, "There are millions of people who care," and he explained to me some of the greatest wisdom I have ever learned.

Mr. Nessen said, "In every town or city in the world, regarding any issue that might exist, there are only 10 people who really matter." He went on to explain that there are movers and shakers that control various areas of interest throughout our society, and for any specific issue, if one of these movers and shakers cared about the Narrative Television Network as much as I did, our problems would be solved. His wisdom was priceless counsel then as it remains today for you and me.

Too many people waste all of their time, effort, and energy telling their stories and making their arguments to the wrong people when they would be much better served to determine who the movers and shakers are and plead their case to those individuals who can really make a difference.

While it remains important who you know, it is critical that you find out what they know and whether they are the people who can solve your problem or help you reach your goal.

As you go through your day today, focus on the critical elements of your goals and the people who can get you there.

Today's the day!

THE MARKET ROLLER COASTER

IN RECENT TIMES, THE REPORTS OF THE STOCK MARKET FLUC-
tuations and economic chaos have made many people rush
from the investment arena in fear. Please note that the stock
market and the economy have not created this fear. The reports
and media hype have created the fear.

Those individuals who have made long-term commitments
to their financial goals and their investments, who have made
the wise decision to not watch the daily financial drama on
cable TV, have experienced little or no anxiety. The market
does not create nearly as much financial risk as is created by
investor anxiety.

Earlier this year, many of the stock market indexes reached
all-time high levels, but then the normal correction cycle set
in and we experienced approximately a 10 percent correction.
Many small retail investors became fearful and jumped out of
the market at the bottom. Then, once the market approached
record territory again, they felt a degree of security returning
and bought back into the market.

The first lesson in the proverbial investment 101 class would
be *buy low and sell high*, but fearful investors continually buy

high and sell low. A hypothetical example from the world's worst investor may help clarify how you should think about the next economic downturn.

Let's call our hero Bob the Bad Investor. Bob began his working career over 40 years ago and determined to periodically invest his earnings in the stock market and leave it there until he retired; but Bob the Bad Investor had the worst timing imaginable. Bob got inspired to begin investing in late 1973 and invested $6,000 just before the market lost 48 percent of its value. He simply held on and hoped for the best. After saving some more money, Bob got up his courage again in 1987 when he invested $46,000 one day before a 34 percent crash in the market. Bob licked his wounds for the next 14 years until he got up the courage to make his final two investments. In 2000, he invested $68,000; and then again in 2007, he invested $64,000—each time entering the market just before the worst downturns in recent history.

Overall, Bob—through his four deposits into his brokerage account—had invested $184,000 throughout his working life. This represents slightly over $10 per day, but unfortunately Bob had saved his money and invested it in lump sums on the four worst days in the market during his lifetime. Some would call Bob a loser while others might call him the unluckiest man alive, but I would call Bob the Bad Investor a millionaire because by investing slightly over $10 per day into a standard market index with the worst possible timing, Bob retired with a nest egg of $1.16 million.

While Bob was, indeed, a bad investor, he is far better off than he would have been if—after losing nearly half of his

$6,000 investment in 1973—he had surrendered to fear and never invested again.

As you go through your day today, be governed by your investment goals and dreams—not fear.

Today's the day!

GOOD DEEDS AND MOTIVES

ALL OF US WOULD LIKE TO THINK WE HAVE HIGH IDEALS AND pure motives. We would tell ourselves that we always do the right things regardless who we are dealing with, but this is, quite simply, not the case. We human beings are not nearly as logical and unaffected by emotion as we would like to believe.

In a recent psychological study, wallets were dropped throughout a major city in subways, on sidewalks, and throughout various business locations in order to see whether the random citizens who happened to come across those wallets would return them. The wallets were identical except for one detail. The variable was the photo that was displayed in the window when the wallet was opened.

Fifteen percent of wallets that had no picture at all were returned, but if the wallets had photos, a higher percentage were returned. This might make sense if you consider that the person who found the wallet could relate better to a photo than a wallet that did not have a personal photograph.

Twenty-five percent of wallets showing an elderly couple were returned. While this might restore your faith in human nature, it doesn't only matter whether or not there's a photo, but it matters greatly whose photo it is.

Forty-eight percent of wallets with a photo of a family were returned. We might assume from this that those who found the wallets showing a family were twice as likely to return those wallets because that family might have more expenses with kids to raise, college educations to save for, and all of the money pressures that families experience.

This human-shared emotion is compelling and would indicate that we all look out for the welfare of one another until you understand that 53 percent of wallets that displayed a picture of a puppy were returned to their owners. An initial observation of this fact might lead one to believe that a photo of a puppy indicates that the owner of the wallet is a loving, caring person; however, the emotional pull created by the photo of the puppy pales in comparison to the emotion demonstrated by the fact that 88 percent of wallets with a photo of a baby were returned.

While it's always dangerous to over-simplify or hyper-analyze psychological studies, it is important to realize that giving people an image to relate to can generate from nearly twice as many results up to almost six times the response. Our message is important and how we communicate it is also important, but who delivers our message may be the most critical component of all.

As you go through your day today, remember that when you want to motivate people, a picture is worth a thousand words.

Today's the day!

Common Millionaires

MANY OF US GREW UP WITH IMAGES OF MILLIONAIRES AS RARE and unusual people. Movies and television depicted millionaires as untouchable and unapproachable individuals who common folk could never meet. Here in the 21st century, economic conditions along with the availability of pre-tax investing for everyone have created an environment where millionaires are commonplace. If you stand on a street corner and inquire of everyone who passes by if they are a millionaire or a school teacher, you will find that you are three times more likely to meet a millionaire than a school teacher.

Today in America, there are over 10 million millionaires. While a million dollars won't buy the lifestyle it would have bought for our grandparents, it's certainly better to have a million dollars than to not have a million dollars. Becoming a millionaire is no longer a matter of winning the gene-pool lottery and inheriting your money, or writing a best seller, signing an NBA contract, or developing a cure for cancer. Becoming a millionaire today is within the reach of almost everyone, but this certainly doesn't mean that the millionaire lifestyle will be lived by everyone.

When I began my working career, I started as an investment broker for a New York Stock Exchange firm. My clients quickly educated me to a reality I had not known before. Looking and acting like a millionaire doesn't make you a millionaire. I had clients who came to my office in brand new luxury automobiles and who lived at the best addresses in town who had low account balances and were constantly borrowing money against their investments to cover expenses. On the other hand, I had clients driving 10-year-old cars, who lived in very nice but moderate housing, and dressed casually who were multimillionaires with a net worth their friends and neighbors would never have imagined.

Trying to look and act like a millionaire before you are one is financially devastating. Farmers who grow corn harvest their crops each year, and those kernels of corn represent not only the product they produce and sell but the seeds they will plant next year. Prevailing wisdom among farmers and wise investors would implore us to "never eat your seed corn."

Particularly as a young person, spending beyond one's means instead of investing creates financial disaster. That expensive pair of shoes, oversized car payment, or bit of bling that could otherwise have been an investment would have generated a fortune in the market throughout an investing life.

Financial success is a matter of thinking more of your own financial future than how much you care about what others may think of your current financial condition. Just as common sense will never be common, wealth will never be average. It's a journey available to everyone but remains the road less traveled.

As you go through your day today, make uncommon decisions now so you can live an uncommon life later.

Today's the day!

ABOUT THE AUTHOR

JIM STOVALL is the president of Narrative Television Network, as well as a published author of many books including *The Ultimate Gift*. He is also a columnist and motivational speaker. He may be reached at 5840 South Memorial Drive, Suite 312, Tulsa, OK 74145-9082; by email at Jim@JimStovall.com; on Twitter at www.twitter.com/stovallauthor; or on Facebook at www.facebook.com/jimstovallauthor.

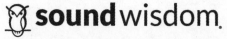

 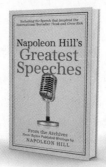